A LIFE:

FROM CHICAGO TO BERKELEY

TO COLORADO SPRINGS

DICK MALKIN

Dedication

This work is written in the memory of my son, Daniel Malkin, and my wife, Carole Malkin

CONTENTS

Introduction	4
Part I. Chicago	5
1. Early Life	
2. Moving and Teenage Years	14
3. College Years	20
Part II. Berkeley	31
1. 1962--67--Graduate School	
2. 1967-69--Sweden	37
3. Back to Berkeley--The 1970s	47
4. Berkeley--The 1980s: Health Problems and Academic Politics	59
5. Berkeley--The 1990s: Teaching and More Health Problems	69
6. Berkeley--2000 and on: Moving towards Retirement	85
Part III. On to Colorado: 2012	98
Part IV. Final Remarks	112
Acknowledgements	114

Introduction

Why am I writing this? I have just finished going through Carole's writings, including novels, short stories and poetry, and I have had several published works that are now available on the Web and will hopefully be there for years and possibly generations. I carried out this little project so that future generations would be able to find and read her writings and, hopefully from this, get a better understanding of her as a creative writer. I would like to add my story to this list of work that covers my life as well. I do not consider myself as famous or particularly special in any way but I think there are aspects of any individual's life that are worth describing, particularly to future family members, such as great grandchildren and beyond, who probably will not have had direct contact with me. I hope they will find something of value for their own lives as they read this.

Part I-Chicago

1. Early life

I was born on March 25, 1940 in Chicago. At this point I must insert a point of fact that will affect all of what follows. I have a very poor memory and when it comes to my early years, there is little detail that is available. However, things do get better as I get to my teenage years and beyond.

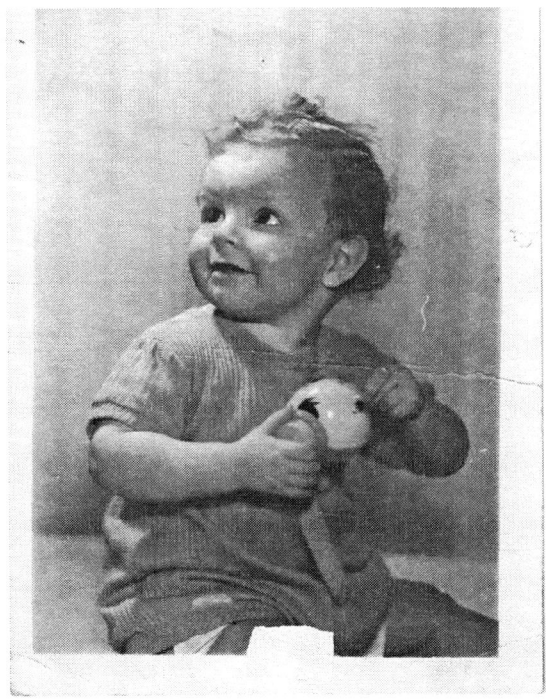

Approx. 6 months old

Some background is necessary. My family consisted of my Mom, Phyllis, my dad, Maurice, and my older brother, Lawrence or Lorry as he was called. Lorry was almost 9 years older than me, which makes me wonder if I was an after-thought child. My mom was a stay-at-home mother in that she did not work when I was growing up, but helped my dad in his later years. My dad owned a liquor store, Ashland Liquors, which had a bar but also sold liquor to take out. In my teenage years, I remember him going to the store very early, such as 6AM and I asked him why he had to go that early. He told me that there were always people who had to drink any time of the day.

Lorry and Dick (approx. 9 months old)

We lived on the far west side of Chicago at 4344 West 14th Street, near Cicero, which was supposed to be a pretty rough area. It was a mixed middle class neighborhood, filled with three story apartment buildings. There was a substantial Jewish community but although my grandfather on my father's side, who I never knew, was a rabbi, we were not a very religious Jewish family. I remember we were on the second floor and there was a small porch off some back stairs and the porch overlooked an empty lot that was called the Poor Farm. In summer, the weeds in the Poor Farm grew so high that we could play in them and you could get lost among them. The most noteworthy site near our apartment, essentially across the street, was Franklin Park, a very large park with playing fields and a swimming pool. In those days, because of polio, no one really went swimming in the summer even though that was the time when the pool would have been most enjoyable. As you will find out later, Franklin Park was the site of a major event in my early life.

A few important things in my early years that I do remember: Probably my earliest memory from those years was the day President Roosevelt died in 1945. People were coming out of their apartments onto their small porches yelling at each other, "The President is dead." Please recall this was a time before the "instant communication" we now have and the best we could do was the party-line-telephone. Secondly, I remember that Lorry had to walk me to Bryant School when I was going to kindergarten. I know he hated doing this because it prevented him from walking with his friends, who were much more important than a five year old little brother. If I wonder why we were not particularly close through those years, I still think that having to walk me to school was one of the important factors.

Approx. 4 years old

When I was nine years old, Franklin Park came into play again, beyond being a place where I played a lot of softball. It was New Year's Day and a neighbor of ours was the first one to get a television set. My family was going to go over and see this remarkable thing, but I did not want to go. Instead I decided to go over to Franklin Park. In the winter, they used to flood the baseball fields and other areas and use them for ice-skating. I never could ice skate so it was not a place you would have thought I would go, particularly on a cold January day. I remember that a group of teen-age boys were on ice, horsing around. For some reason they decided to pick on me and, in fact, one of them actually picked me up and that's when things got out of control. He raised me over his head and then dropped me. Bad luck for me. I landed on my face, which was immediately a bloody mess. I don't really remember all that happened next but I know I was taken to an emergency room and examined. The doctor told my mom he did not think I had a broken nose, and that was how it was left. After all the swelling and black-and blue decreased, one look at my face gave a clear picture that my nose was crooked and that I had broken my nose in the fall. This became my badge of honor during my teen-age years, but my mom had a thing about noses and it was not unusual for her to comment of people's noses that were "a little bit off." This is an introduction to an on-going saga that went on for years and that I will return to as I deal with my high school years.

Franklin Park-approx. 8 years old

Another quite amusing story of my younger life concerned my feet and my mother's attempts to correct all my little infirmities. My mother somehow got the idea that I had flat feet and she wanted to have this corrected. I remember taking the streetcar down Roosevelt Road all the way downtown to see a specialist foot doctor. He probably was a podiatrist and he said he had "special shoes" that I should wear all the time. These shoes are what I would call "old man" shoes but they also contained these steel sections that held my feet firmly in place. They were expensive and ugly. Not exactly what an 8 year old wanted to wear to school and around. They were heavy, and I mean really heavy so that it was a challenge to run and jump with them. I wore them through all of high school and they really didn't do much for my feet. One of the first things I did when I went off to college was throw them out and get a pair of loafers, something I coveted all through high school since these were what the "cool" guys were wearing. This is just another example of what my mom did for me because I did not come up to her idea of perfection.

One thing we never did as a family was take vacations. We did, on some occasions, go to the beach in Chicago or nearby Indiana, but even that was not often because my dad was very light-skinned and if he sat in the sun for 5 minutes, he turned beet-red. I remember him once going to the beach in a long bath robe, every thing covered up except for about a two inch part of his lower legs, right above his ankles. And, of course, when we went home that little stretch of skin was sunburned. So, how then did we get to go on a rather long road trip one summer that took us to the East coast? The whole family drove from Chicago, across Michigan and Ontario, Canada, to reach Niagara Falls then on to a place that I thought I would never visit: Cooperstown, New York, home of the Baseball Hall of Fame. I was an avid baseball fan and seeing the Hall was like going to the Vatican for a Catholic. We went on to Brooklyn where one of my mother's brothers lived. Uncle Albert and his family were so lively and different than my family. Albert had two daughters, Marlene and Dorothy, who were outspoken about everyone and every thing.

They lived near Ebbets Field, home of the Brooklyn Dodgers, and any time there was a home game, we were practically at the game since we could hear all the cheering. We did all the tourist things with my cousins: Statue of Liberty, Empire State Building, etc., and for me it was like being in another world. From New York, we drove to Washington, D. C., and again were full and complete tourists. We then went on to Cleveland, where one of my mom's two sisters, Dinah, lived. She was married to Morris Milstein, who owned the largest Oldsmobile agency in Cleveland. Unfortunately, things took a bad turn when we were in Cleveland. My dad suddenly took sick and it turned out he had a stroke. He was never a healthy individual, was somewhat overweight and was a regular smoker.

      The stroke affected our family for the rest of our lives. My father recovered although he always walked with a slight limp. Most critical for his future life was that he was not allowed to drive. My mom, who never learned to drive before my dad's stroke, became his driver and he was entirely dependent on her. She had to drive him to work every morning and pick him up every evening. On top of this, she was not a particularly good driver and it was always nerve-racking to be in the car when she was behind the wheel. All of this had a dramatic effect on my parent's relationship, which I noticed over my teen years. Simply put, she was not very nice

Family Picture in Cleveland. 1948-8 years old

to my dad, always criticizing him for little things she did not like, and there was always a level of anxiety around the house. Ours was not a close family where problems were brought into the open and discussed. If I did something that was not acceptable, I would get a stone cold look from my mom and that was that. This was more than enough to know she was displeased She did not interact with me very much and I was on my own once I started high school. The cool and distant relationship persisted through out my adult life. I believe it was based on her relationship with my father after so many responsibilities fell upon her.

2. Moving and Teenage years

In 1951, I was eleven years old and there was another major event in our family life. At that time, we moved from the West side of Chicago to South Shore, which was a more upscale neighborhood on the South side. South Shore contains a large number of apartment buildings but there were also single-family homes, giving a picture of affluence. We lived in an apartment at 7746 Yates Avenue and although there were only two bedrooms, it was a much larger apartment than the West side apartment. One important factor in this move was that almost all of my dad's family, his brothers and sisters, lived in South Shore. Although not a close family, there was more contact among family members in South Shore, and I remember the once a month "cousins club" where everyone got together for socializing.

At the time of this move, Lorry was almost 20 years old and was thought to be too old to share a bedroom with his little brother. The apartment had an enclosed porch off his bedroom and this became my bedroom. There was one big problem that no on considered: there was no heat in the porch and I need not tell you that it gets very cold in Chicago in the winter. Lorry took pity on me and one day an electric blanket appeared that probably saved my life.

After two years at Bradwell School, I moved on to high school at South Shore High School. In those days, there were not any junior high schools in Chicago, only 8 years in your elementary school and four years in high school. The South Shore area was heavily Jewish and this could also be seen in South Shore High, which was over 90% Jewish. Friendships were easy among the students and I had 6-8 good friends who spent most of their out of school time together. We would rotate from home to home and thus got to know entire families. My friends were welcome at my home, but they quickly learned that my mother was an immaculate housekeeper and dirt was not allowed in. So, when they came to my house, shoes had to be removed at the front door and you were forced to sit on plastic slipcovers on the chairs and davenport (sofa was not an acceptable term) if you came over. There was nothing more awful than plastic slipcovers in a Chicago summer (we never had air conditioning).

My high school years were easy and enjoyable. I did not spend much time studying but I always got excellent grades. My mom pretty much left me alone since she was working with my dad in the liquor store. We were a group of kids who were not looking for trouble and just enjoyed hanging out or playing basketball outside someone's house. One thing we were not into was girls, and none of this group of guys had any interest in getting involved with girls. This was a time when these two groups just stayed away from each other, at least in South Shore.

Although not seriously religious, my parents insisted I have a Bar Mitzvah when I turned 13. I had gone to a Hebrew school on the West side and it was one of the most horrible experiences of my young life. It was at an Orthodox *shul* and the instructor was one of the rabbis. I still remember his walking around the classroom carrying a long cane that was used to smack the students who were not showing sufficient attention to the subject. I did learn to read Hebrew and could hold my own if we ever went to a holiday service, like Rosh Hashanah or Yom Kippur. I also remember that I played hooky from the West side Hebrew School and would spend the two hours at Zimbler's Deli a few blocks from my house where I loved playing on a pinball machine. When my mom was informed that I was missing class, I paid a very painful price for this transgression. On the South side, the *shul* we attended was Conservative and things were low key so I succeeded in getting through my Bar Mitzvah with no pain.

During the summer of my second year in high school, my friend Al Telser and I had the opportunity to attend a special summer school for high local high school students that was held at the University of Chicago. We would travel to and from the campus by public transportation. We took two classes, one in English and the second in Biology. The class in biology provided me with one of those "gotcha" moments in your life. I remember looking through a microscope for the first time and seeing a world of bacteria swimming around. Other experiments were equally amazing and all of this made me realize that this field of biology was really something I would like to do in my later life. I don't know if the summer was as significant for Al as it was for me, but it turned out that we both went to graduate schools in Biochemistry.

15 years old

Although Lorry and I were not close, there is one thing I am indebted to him for. While I was in high school, our house was filled with classical music due to Lorry's enthusiasm. He listened primarily to orchestral music of all kinds with some additional interest in chamber music. I guess by simple osmosis I too became a classical music buff during those years. Lorry even went so far as to have a subscription to the Chicago Symphony

Orchestra, which took him down to Orchestra Hall in downtown Chicago once a week. On some occasions he could not go to his concert and he would give me his two tickets (he went with a friend). My friend Al was also into the classical scene and we had this opportunity to hear the symphony in person. In those days, the symphony conductor was Fritz Reiner and the orchestra was recognized as one of the two or three best in the country. This interest of mine has been maintained over the years and in more recent times (I call them the mature years), I have become a serious opera enthusiast. More on this later, but I would like to acknowledge the wonderful present that my brother gave me in my teen-age years.

When I was 16, my mom decided something had to be done with my crooked nose. I don't know if she thought there would be some great tragedy that would occur to me because my nose was not straight, but we started to see an ear-nose-throat doctor who recommended I have a "nose job" or rhinoplasty. I must admit that after my nose was broken, I did have problems breathing out of one side of my nose, but this still was not enough to convince anyone that I should not undergo the nose job. But this was a battle I could not win. During the summer of my 16th year, I went to the hospital to have the problem fixed. I remember to this day seeing my mom after the surgery and, as they rolled me out of the operating room, and I was starting to turn black and blue, I said to her "I hope you are satisfied." The result of all of this is that I have had for the past almost 60 years a nose that is not really my nose, but is some doctor's creation. Worse than that, I still can't breathe out of one side of my nose!

    Overall, my high school years were pleasant and undemanding. I was a very good student and this resulted in my parents not bothering me about academic achievement. My mom was obsessed with the idea that I had to become the first medical doctor in the Malkin family. Lorry probably could have done this, but his career bounced around quite a bit and he ended up as a hospital administrator. This put more pressure on me to join the medical profession. Whether I was interested in this or not did not seem to matter, but all of this came to the forefront as I started to think about colleges.

High School graduation-1957

3. College in Yellow Springs

With over 90% of my graduating class being Jewish, this put a lot of pressure on people to go to "good" schools, although many simply went to the University of Illinois in Urbana. My mom decided that I should to the University of Chicago, a top grade institution. I even took an exam for a scholarship there and received a scholarship. However, there was one major problem for me--going to the University of Chicago meant I would live at home and this was not a situation I wanted to be in. I started looking around at other schools and came across

Antioch College in Yellow Springs, Ohio. Antioch was a small liberal arts college in Yellow Springs, Ohio, and twenty-five miles from Dayton in Southern Ohio. Its academic reputation was excellent in those days but it slipped in later years. One thing it had going for it in relation to my situation was that it had a work-study program required for your degree. All students spent 6 months each year on campus taking classes and the 6 months working on a cooperative program job. You needed both class credit and job credits to graduate. Because of the work-study program, it was a five-year program to obtain a BS/BA degree. The college had over the years amassed a large number of jobs available for students, and these were distributed throughout the country. Some jobs, particularly in the hard sciences, were excellent and others were more menial. I was impressed by what I read about Antioch and was even more impressed when one day while at school, I was asked to come down to the college advisor office because there was someone from Antioch who wanted to talk with me about the college. This turned out to be the Admissions Director who provided me with much more information on Antioch. My folks were not enthusiastic about me going to Southern Ohio, but the selling point was that I was going to have real jobs that paid me real salaries while I was working and this would allow me to contribute to the cost of my education. As an aside, tuition at Antioch was $800 per year in 1957. My folks were not into the whole college thing as long as I went somewhere to be a premed and if it was cheaper than other places, this was a good thing. So the decision was made that I would go to Antioch. In those days you didn't go visit schools and do comparative shopping. I was very happy about the decision because I was 300 miles away from home and weekend visits from either party were out.

I am not certain of this, but I think Lorry drove me down to Yellow Springs when I was starting my first year at Antioch. When you enter Yellow Springs, one is taken by how little there is there. Main street had two places frequented by students: The Tavern and The Little Art Theater. The latter was notable for showing high quality foreign movies in the 1950s, and one could look forward to seeing the Swedish films of Ingmar Bergman and the Japanese films of Akira Kurosawa. Off the main street were several side streets, one of which contains the bulk of the college's buildings. In 1957, student life centered around the Student Union, which contained the Cafeteria, the only dining hall on campus where everyone ate. When I came to Antioch, the total enrollment was 1200 students, but on campus, there were about 600 students at any one time since half of the population was on coop jobs. What became obvious very quickly was that you knew pretty much everybody in your year, from either having them in your classes or seeing them at the meal times.

My first year at Antioch was academically very undistinguished. I mentioned that I had not studied very much in high school and that I did fine. Starting out on a premed program put me into chemistry, physics and calculus my first quarter and I did not do very well, particularly in physics and calculus. I had never had physics in high school and struggled, finally realizing I had to do a lot more work than I had in the past. There were few distractions on campus: no sororities or fraternities and no intercollegiate academic activities. The college did have an active music/theater program that brought well-established artists to the campus.

    The most noteworthy activity for me during my first year was my first coop job. I went back to Chicago to work in Michael Reese Hospital as an orderly, a job that my brother helped me get since he was working in the administration of Michael Reese. This job was to fit in with my premedical training, but it had more of a negative effect on me. Since I was on the job for only six months, I rotated with various units, such as obstetrics/gynecology, medical units on different floors and the emergency room. My hours were also shifting and I worked the night shift in ER for one of my longer stints. Working at night in a large hospital is a rather strange experience. It is relatively dark, very quiet and there are not many people around. I certainly remember that one thing I was called on to do at night when I was on the floors and that was to deal with patients who passed away, moving them from their room to the morgue. The ER experience was different. My most notable contribution was to deliver on two occasions babies in the back of a car and a taxi. I still wonder how these two new "patients" would have reacted if they knew a 17 year old college freshman was their delivering "doctor."

My second year at Antioch was much more eventful. My coop job turned out to be an important experience. I went to New York City and worked at the NYU Medical Center as an operating room technician. I was the guy who scrubbed in to surgery and handed the instruments to the surgeon! Again, I was only 18 years old and this was a pretty responsible position. What was important was that I really got to see medicine in action, and for the most important, I was not impressed by what I saw. I found the doctors to be fairly uninteresting individuals who, for many of them, reminded me of plumbers. The rigid system in the OR was also difficult and many of the technical and nursing staff spent their time figuring out how to beat the system, which meant avoiding the chief OR nurse who was the real power in the OR. My real enjoyment came from living in New York in Greenwich Village, and I even had a gay roommate. But at the end of the day, I decided this was a group of people who I did not want to spend my life with and that medicine was not for me.

While this was all very important, something happened in my second year that was even more important and that was that I met Carole. This came about in a rather complex way. I had noticed her in the Cafeteria off and on because she had a striking green outfit: green sweater and skirt. I know this sounds very silly but it made her stand out from her friends. I was very inexperienced with girls although I did manage to get a date for our prom when I graduated from high school. The story now gets more complicated. I lived with a gang of guys who were a little loony. One of them, John, had a car that looked like he had completely rewired. It was February 1958, and four of us decided to drive to New York City for a weekend: 600 miles, at least a 10-hour drive. This was what you did when you were a second year college student who wanted to get out of Yellow Springs.

I do remember the exact date because it was Valentine's Day, February 14, 1958, a Friday. What we decided about the trip was that we would see if we could get two passengers to come along and help pay for the gas. A notice was put up on a board in the Student Union, and two women responded, one going to Philadelphia and the second to New York City. We all met at 3 PM for the trip. It turned out that the New York passenger was Carole. The women were a little shocked when John told them they should be sure to go to the bathroom before we left because we were not planning any "pit stops" on the way. Whether he was serious or not was not clear. Carole later told me that she was a little nervous when she discovered her riding mates were four guys who looked very scruffy.

When you spend 20 hours (coming and going) in a car with people, one does try to make the time pass with chitchat in between napping. My first impression was that Carole was very intelligent and very serious. She was the kind of person who started their term papers the day after the assignment was given instead of waiting to the last minute. But her kindness also came through.

When we arrived back at school early Sunday morning, everyone went their separate ways. About a week later, I saw Carole walking across campus and took up all my courage to go up to her and say hello. I remember that she seemed surprised when I approached her and finally told me that she had seen a couple of the other guys on the trip and said hello but got the so-called "cold shoulder," and she expected the same from me. We chatted for a while and finally I asked her if she would like to go to a concert by Theodore Bikel that was coming up. She said that would be nice and that was the beginning of something that went on for over 50 years.

My third year at Antioch was highlighted by a coop job at MIT with Professor Alexander Rich, a biophysicist. Carole also had a coop job in the Boston area, in Newton, MA, where she was a teaching assistant at a Newton elementary school. I had a little apartment in Cambridge and Carole lived close by with another Antioch student. We saw a lot of each other during this 3-month job period. While at school, I firmly decided that medicine was not in my future and became chemistry major. The chemistry program at Antioch was small, with only 5 chemistry majors in my year. The faculty was excellent and it was quite an experience to take the same courses with the same 4 other students all the time.

1960-Washington, D. C.

In the fall of 1960, we decided we wanted to get married. We had wanted to get married in Yellow Springs, but Carole was not old enough so at the last minute we dashed off to New York where we were both "of age." We were very young (I was 20 and Carole 18) but by that time we were sure that we wanted to be together. My parents were shocked when we told them. They had met Carole once at Thanksgiving, but had no idea what was going to happen to us. My mom thought I would quit school and she was calmed down when I told her I had no such plan and would finish Antioch and then go on to graduate school in biochemistry. For various bureaucratic reasons, we ended up getting married in Brooklyn at Carole's aunt's apartment on December 25, 1960, in a wedding performed by an Orthodox rabbi who had been an instructor at a Hebrew school Carole briefly attended. Carole's brother Norman had made a reservation for us at the Waldorf Astoria in New York City so we had the experience of staying at a world-class hotel after our wedding.

      Shortly after the wedding, we went on to Washington, D.C. for our next coop jobs. We were fortunate in that both Carole and I had jobs at the National Institutes of Health in Bethesda, MD. Carole worked with a sociologist in the Mental Health Institute and I worked with Dr. Darwin Prockop in a medical institute. These turned out to be excellent jobs, giving us hands-on experience in our major fields of study at Antioch. We lived in Washington near DuPont Circle and enjoyed the cultural scene and even got to go to the Inauguration Celebration for President Kennedy in January, 1960.

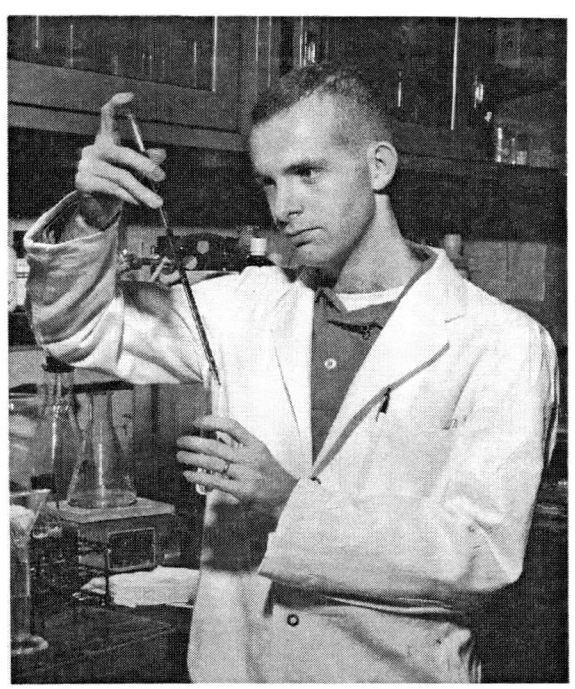

National Institutes of Health-1960

As we moved towards graduation at Antioch (Carole was one year behind me and finished her requirements after we left for California), things were much quieter. We moved off-campus as a married couple and lived at the back of an old house with two rooms, one of the first floor and the other on the second floor. The main activity for me was to sort out graduate schools. My decision to go into biochemistry held firm, and I looked at various programs around the country. To appease my parents, I had to apply to the University of Chicago where they had a good program, but there was no way I was going there. I applied to five schools and got into all but Stanford. The chairman of the

Chemistry Department at Antioch had a friend in the Biochemistry Department at UC Berkeley and he strongly recommended their program. When it came down to a decision, I remember saying that neither of us had been west of the Mississippi River and maybe it was time to go west. The department in Berkeley looked to have a large number of excellent people as well, and that sealed the decision.

Part II-Berkeley

1. 1962-1967: Graduate School

We spent over 40 years in Berkeley and many personal events of high significance occurred over this period, from getting a Ph.D. in biochemistry to a postdoctoral period in Sweden, then back to Berkeley to become a faculty member at UC Berkeley. This long a span in any one's life is filled with good and bad, and we had our share of both, and you will find them filled out for you in this second section.

When we decided to go to California, one early question was how were we going to get there. Fortunately, Carole was working at Wright-Patterson Airbase right before we left and she put up a note on community bulletin board: "If you have a car that needs transporting to California, we would love to drive it there for you." Magically, we got a call from a colonel in the Air Force who was being transferred to Southern California and had a second car that he would like to have driven. The details were worked out and we were able to drive from Ohio to Berkeley in his car, packed up with everything we owned. I still remember getting off the freeway exit at University Avenue, driving up that street and wondering where the University was. As we neared the Berkeley hills, we could see the Campanile and we knew we were just about there.

I don't remember how we found a place to live, but we were very lucky to find a very nice apartment in an older apartment on Le Conte Avenue, one block from the campus and less than a 10 minute walk to the Biochemistry Building. Our one bedroom apartment was at the back of the first floor, overlooking a small garden with an apricot tree in the middle. The apartment was quite nice, with beams in the living room ceiling. The rent was $70 per month. These were the good old days.

After returning the car to the colonel in Southern California, we settled into the academic year. Carole was taking an Italian class on campus so that she could finish her Antioch requirements and I was involved in learning some biochemistry. The atmosphere in the department was low key and supportive, and there new students seemed like a reasonable, friendly group. It was interesting some of the faculty seemed to think my "preparation" was not "up to snuff" since I came from a small school in Ohio that many did not know very much about. But I found many of the first year courses to actually be less difficult than my undergraduate chemistry courses, and I did just fine in the Berkeley classes.

As my first year progressed, there were two important activities in which I became involved. Firstly, there was my Ph.D. qualifying examination that would be taken in the second year. Secondly, there was the choice of a research laboratory in which I would do my Ph.D. research project. The qualifying exam situation was clear in that I had to prepare two research proposals and defend them in front of five faculty members. It turned out that my exam, which I took in my 4th semester, was no problem at all. The choice of a lab was more difficult. When I came to Berkeley, I was interest in enzymes, the somewhat magical proteins in the cell that were involved in all metabolic activities. The question about these proteins was very simple-- how did they carry out their reactions? The way you sought out a lab was firstly to talk to the prospective faculty member about their work and then possibly talk to other students already in the lab about what it is like working for this professor. There were a few faculty involved in studies of enzymes but for one reason or another, their work did not interest me. I also met some third and fourth year graduate students at the daily coffee hour that the department held, where students and faculty would get together in an informal setting and talk over anything that was going on in the department. At these coffee hours, I met Professor Jesse Rabinowitz and talked with him about his work. One thing I liked about Jesse was his informality: everyone called him by his first name, in contrast to some faculty who had to referred to as Professor or Doctor. I knew absolutely nothing about the work Jesse was doing. It involved folic acid metabolism in anaerobic bacteria, but after talking with some of his students, I got a good feeling about his lab, how it was "managed" and how there was an enormous amount of cooperation among all of the staff and students in the lab. The several graduate students in the lab thought highly of Jesse as a research supervisor and they felt his work was always of the highest quality. No one had a bad word to say about him. So, I put my love of enzymes aside and went to work in the area of bacterial metabolism. In retrospect, it was one of wisest decisions I ever made, besides getting married to Carole when I was 20. I was happy to receive an NIH predoctoral fellowship that paid $3000 per year, so I did not have to worry about the cost of my training.

When I started working in Jesse's lab, there were postdoctoral fellows in the lab: Ko Uyeda, Walt Lowenbeg and Bob Buchanan. There were also two other more senior graduate students in the lab: Ted Chase and Sam Raeburn. Carole and I became good friends with Sam over the years and maintained contact even after he left Berkeley. Sam had been a child artist prodigy and ultimately gave up being a scientist for his painting. Sam had studied Chinese before coming to Berkeley as a biochemistry graduate student, and it was always fun to go to Oakland Chinatown and watch him shock the waiter/waitress by ordering in Chinese. We always got great service when this happened.

Another first year student came into Jesse's lab at the same time. He was Ben Tonomura, a student who had come to Berkeley from Japan. Ben was rather quiet, possibly due to the new culture he was encountering, but he was a warm and helpful person. He and I were assigned a project when we first came into the lab for our first summer of research. We worked with some unusual anaerobic bacteria that produced methane gas. These bacteria were supposed to be very primitive and difficult to grow in cultures, but we successfully grew them in large bottles and looked at the composition of their DNA. The results were of enough interest that we were able to report them in a short paper in the Journal of Bacteriology. It was quite an accomplishment for first year students to publish and I think we were the envy of our class. Ben returned to Kyoto, Japan after getting his Ph.D. and Carole and I had the opportunity to have dinner with him many years later on a trip we took to Japan.

    I was extremely lucky in my thesis research project. I had come into the lab shortly after a new type of iron-containing protein had been discovered in the type of anaerobic bacteria that we worked on. The protein had been named ferredoxin, relating to the fact that it contained iron ("ferre) and underwent oxidation-reduction reactions ("redoxin"). Little was known about the chemical structure of this protein and this became the focus of my research. Over the next two years, I did a series of experiments that resulted in our understanding of how the iron was bound in the protein and the identification of a new form of sulfur, acid-labile sulfide that was also present. Several publications appeared from this work in major biochemistry journals. As I was finishing up, Jesse had been invited to submit a review on the ferredoxin type of proteins, and he asked me to co-author this article since I could also use it as an introductory chapter for my thesis. The article entitled "Non-heme iron electron transfer proteins" was published in the Annual Review of Biochemistry in 1967, and was a most fitting completion for my Ph.D. degree.

As an aside, I should mention that during the time I was a graduate student, the so-called Free Speech Movement occurred. This was the first major uprising at a large American university. Although not directly involved, one could not avoid being swept up by what was happening: the initial demonstration in Sproul Plaza with Mario Savio speaking from the top of UC police car, the tear gas rolling across the campus as the police tried to break up rallies, the National Guard, called out by Governor Reagan, lining various pathways around the campus and standing rigidly in line with their rifles and bayonets, and a large open rally at the Greek Theater where the UC police physically removed Savio from the stage in front of 13,000 students. Since we were at the opposite end of the campus from where all the demonstrations were occurring, there was little direct effect and it is hard to imagine that we continued working in the lab through much of the hubbub.

Another strong memory that I have--November 22, 1963, a Friday afternoon. Ted Chase had a radio in the lab and it usually had music on, but an announcement came on saying that President Kennedy had been shot in Dallas. Everything stopped and we sat around that little radio until we heard he had been assassinated after which people just quietly went home. The rest of the weekend was unreal and it took some time for everyone to get back to a normal life.

2. 1967-1969: Sweden

As I was nearing the end of my thesis work, I began to consider what would come next in my career. I was interested in metallo-proteins, that is, proteins that contained metal ions as part of their structure, and I wanted to continue in this field. It is a rather specialized area in the general area of protein biochemistry, but there were labs in the US and abroad that were attractive. I particularly wanted to go to a lab that specialized in studying this group of proteins using highly sophisticated physical spectroscopic methods, and one lab that was highly recognized was in the Biochemistry Department of the University of Goteborg in Sweden with Professor Bo Malmstrom as head. I contacted Professor Malmstrom and was accepted as a post-doctoral fellow in the lab. I was also very fortunate to obtain my own funding for this two-year postdoc, with funds from NATO and the American Cancer Society.

I also must apologize for having to backtrack a little to mention another important event in Carole and my life. On June 29, 1963, our son Daniel was born at Herrick Hospital in Berkeley. Carole used two gynecologists for this pregnancy, and this was amusing because they were twins and you never knew which one was treating you. Carole used "natural childbirth", the so-called Lamaze method, and everything went very well. Our good friend, Sam, drove us home from the hospital and he was a nervous wreck in the car. He honked at every car within 100 yards of us and kept muttering, "Don't they know there's a new baby in this car?" We were excited at becoming parents and

Daniel (3 months old) and his parents -1963

Carole was a wonderful mother taking care of the new infant. We had to move to a new larger apartment because of the increase in family size and moved to a flat that was the second floor of a house on Hearst Avenue. This place was much larger than the La Loma apartment and had access to a large back yard.

It was also near Totland Park where we would take Daniel for outings. Carole met many friends at Totland, some of whom became very close over the years. I should also mention that my parents in Chicago thought I should come to Chicago for post-doctoral work and were quite shocked when I told them we were going to Sweden.

I completed my degree requirements in early 1967 and thought that since I was now a Ph.D., I should be paid as a Ph.D. Unfortunately, Jesse did not agree and he said he did not have the money. We then decided to do something totally radical. We would go to Europe in April, purchase a VW bus, and travel around Europe until mid-August when we were supposed to arrive in Gothenburg. It was to be The Grand Tour.

Passport-1967

We left Berkeley, stopped in Chicago for a few days and then flew directly to Munich where we picked up our VW van. I remember that the jet lag was terrible and that we had to spend a great deal of time driving around Munich trying to find our campground. The weather was also miserable, as it was cold and rainy. Not a good start to our trip. But we managed as I learned what the road signs in Europe meant and that I should never get in the fast lane on the Autobahn with a VW bus. We then went to Salzburg and Mozart's house where Daniel, who was not quite 4 years old, insisted he had seen Mozart there. There was a very old Austrian woman at the entrance and her grey hair did look like Mozart's in many pictures on records that I owned but when we explained this to Daniel, he was insistent that he saw Mozart.

    We drove through the Alps into Italy and spent the next five weeks traveling up and down Italy. There was not much we missed and we loved the Italians. They were very taken by the fact that we were traveling with such a young child. We quickly learned how to manage our car. Carole and I slept in the rear of the bus and there was a stiff hammock that stretched out over the front seats where Daniel slept. He turned out to be a terrific traveler, spending time in the books with his Batman comic books while we drove through Italy. I think we saw so many churches that we lost count. Daniel got very good at identifying the religious pictures that were present throughout Italy. One amusing incident: we went up Mount Vesuvius outside Naples and we told Daniel the story of Pompeii, which was not very smart of us since he was convinced the volcano was going to erupt again while we were on it.

From Italy, we traveled along the Riviera through Nice and Cannes and then started moving north. One special meal was at a two star Michelin restaurant in Avignon with Daniel sitting on the floor under the table reading his comic books. We decided to go through Switzerland instead of straight north. Our destination was really Paris but as we often did on the trip, we never went by the shortest route. We had gotten pretty good at finding grounds and did not spend one night in a hotel on the entire trip. A strong memory of Paris: it turned out that we were in Paris on June 29th, Daniel's 4th birthday. We wanted to do something special and bought a cake and candles, took these things up to the top of the Eiffel Tower and celebrated. The guards and tourists all joined in for a most unusual event. We spent a great deal of time in and around Paris, including the Loire Valley, Versailles and on and on. After Paris we again went north through Normandy and the allied war cemeteries. Belgium, Holland was particularly beautiful and we met some warm Dutch people at the campground in Holland. Northern Germany was next as we were inching closer to Sweden. Finally, Denmark and Tivoli were the last of Northern Europe before taking a ferry to Gothenburg. I am not doing justice to this trip, which turned out to be a memorable experience for all of us, and it was the trip of a lifetime.

Our arrival in Gothenburg was very smooth. We had rented an apartment in a high-rise building that was about a 20 minute walk from the lab so that I could walk to and from even in the winter. This building was typical of Swedish housing where there are few individual homes and many multi-floor apartment buildings. I assume this is because it is more energy efficient to not have so many one family homes. One notable event happened shortly after we arrived. The Swedish driving system was like the one in England. That is, they drove on the "wrong" side of the road in comparison to most of the rest of the world. Some time ago, the decided to change over and drive on the right, not the left and this happened two weeks after we arrived. What was amazing was how they carried out this transition over a single weekend. All roads and streets were shut down for two days to do whatever final modifications had to be made. There were no cars, busses, etc. moving on a Saturday and Sunday and then on Monday, you could drive again, but, only with a 20 mile per hour speed limit. What surprised me was how many people climbed into their cars on Monday morning to try to the new system, and amazingly, it all went smoothly.

I started working in the lab right after getting settled and there was more settling that had to be done. Meeting new people, finding out where everything was and on and on. There was another American in the lab, Jim Fee, who had come about six months before me and helped me out getting adjusted to the Swedes and the Swedish system. People at work were friendly and the senior scientists were all comfortable with English, while some of the staff were a little hesitant to converse in English. I had decided on a project before I arrived but after a couple of weeks I changed my mind and moved on to a second project. The main research interest in the lab dealt with the structure of proteins that contained copper. Some of these proteins were enzymes that reacted with oxygen in a complex series of reactions. The enzymes were nicknamed "blue copper proteins" because of their intense blue color that came from the metal in the protein. Little was known about how the copper was bound in the protein or how it functioned, so there was much to do.

    I worked closely with one of the biophysicists in the group, Tore Vanngard. Tore was intelligent, kind and patient, and an excellent scientific mentor. Tore used sophisticated physical techniques to study metal ions in proteins, and once I learned how to used these instruments, I had complete access to them. What was exceptional was his ability to interpret the data that I would obtain and even though I achieved some level of confidence in this area, it only came about after working with someone who had years of experience in this area.

    In the first few months in Gothenburg, my progress was slow and I did not have any substantial results. At one point, after about 6 months, I even considered leaving Sweden and returning to the US and I discussed this with Carole. She was heavily involved in taking care of Daniel and the apartment and doing most of this in Swedish. Daniel had started in a play school and had made numerous friends. As Carole had done in Berkeley, she became friends with some of the mothers. After a few months, Daniel was fluent in Swedish, with no accent, so that when we went out, he and Carole did the talking. Making friends was difficult for me, primarily because the Swedes are not the most social of people. It was not unusual for people in our building to close the elevator doors if they saw us coming.

Two things occurred in the early months of 1968. In February, Lorry called me to tell that our father had passed away. As I mentioned before, he was not a well man, but it still came as a surprise because I was not aware he was ill in any way. For various reasons, I could not go to Chicago for the funeral. One reason for this was that Carole was pregnant, expecting a baby in early April, and I did not think I should leave her alone at this time. On April 2, 1968, at a local hospital in Gothenburg Carole had a baby girl who was named Karin Annika, a very Swedish name. It was quite amusing when I received a call from some church asking me if I wanted to have my new daughter baptized. Apparently everyone born in Sweden is automatically a member of the Lutheran church, but I told the caller I had to decline this request because we were

Jewish and we were not Swedish citizens. The caller sounded surprised, but at least he did not try to convince me of a serious mistake in judgment.

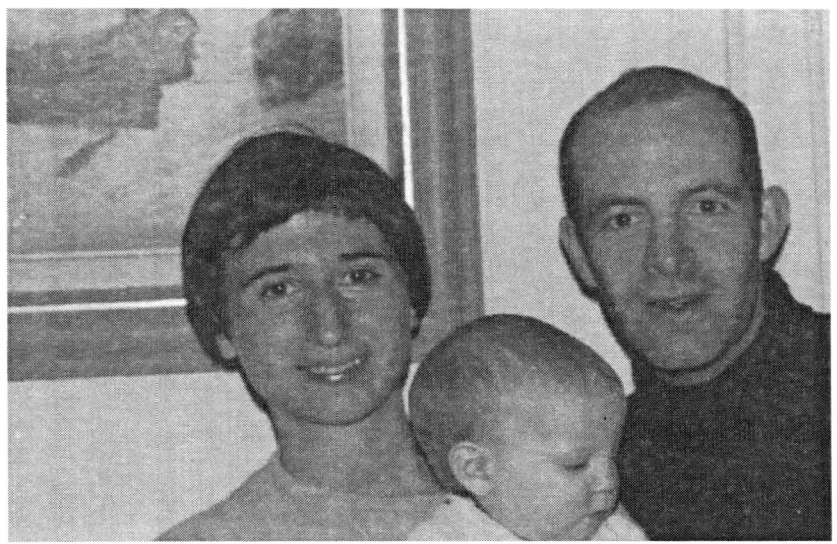

Karin and parents-Sweden 1968

After some time in the lab, I started to work more closely with Tore Vanngard, a biophysicist. Tore was an excellent scientist and an excellent human being and it was a privilege to work with him. My research progress was much better and it was a good decision to stay a second year in the lab. I had some very good publications and I was invited to attend a Gordon Conference in the summer of 1968. The title of the Conference was "Metal Ions in Biology" and it covered a broad range of topics related to my graduate student and post-doctoral work.

The Gordon Conferences are held in the summer at unused prep schools in New Hampshire and are famous for bringing leading scientists together in a very informal setting. I made two key contacts at the conference. First, Bob Buchanan, a postdoc in Jesse's lab when I was a graduate student, was there. He had finished his postdoc period in the lab and had a position the Department of Cell Physiology on campus. I was not familiar with this department but he explained to me that it was a unit that functioned more like a research center than a regular academic department and that everyone in the unit was studying photosynthesis. Professor Dan Arnon, who was famous for his discovery of photosynthetic phosphorylation, ran the department. Bob told me there was a great interest in copper proteins among the lab members and perhaps something could be worked out for me to return to Berkeley in Cell Physiology. Of course, this was very exciting since at this time it was not clear what I would do when I left Sweden. The second was with Alan Bearden, who was a biophysicist at UC San Diego and was moving to Berkeley in the Biophysics unit as a faculty member. His expertise involved spectroscopy and we discussed possible joint projects if I did return to Berkeley. So when I returned to Sweden after the conference, I felt it had been an extremely useful trip.

We enjoyed out second year more than the first one. I guess we were more comfortable with the lifestyle of the

Swedes, with not very high expectations for making good friends. My work in the lab had also picked up and it looked like I would get some good publications out. In the spring of 1969, we had the opportunity to go to a meeting in Madrid and Carole and I packed up the kids and had an adventure. Karin was only a little more than a year old but she did well. After a rough Swedish winter, it was a joy to see the sun and feel the warmth of Southern Europe.

3. Back to Berkeley: the 1970s

When we returned to Berkeley in the summer of 1969, we had no idea we would be living there for the next 43 years. We immediately rented a small house on Hearst Avenue, not far from where we had lived two years ago. The house was rather small but convenient to the Cell Physiology Department located near the Oxford-Hearst Avenue corner. The Department was located in Hilgard Hall, one of older buildings on the campus and a building that barely suitable for research work in modern biochemistry. There was no air conditioning and during the warm summer afternoons, the sun from the west would pour into our lab rooms, making them unbearably hot. While the labs had been remodeled to some degree in the early 1960s, they provided a challenge to getting things done.

When I came to the department, I had been appointed as research scientist in the Agricultural Experiment Station. I had no idea what this meant other than I was not to be paid on "soft" money from a research grant, but the University, even though this was not a regular faculty position. With time I understood this situation very well. The department was strange. There was only one regular faculty member and that was Professor Arnon. Then there was a staff of some 6-8 Ph.D.'s being supported as I was or from research grants to Professor Arnon. Since none of us were regular faculty, we could not obtain funding from outside sources. There were also 3-4 technical staff that either worked on their own projects under Professor Arnon's supervision or supported the Ph.Ds. The unusual thing was that all of the Ph.D.'s had their own projects but they worked directly under the supervision of Professor Arnon. There were no students in the department and the department taught no courses. The atmosphere was very European with Professor Arnon making the rounds in the morning, visiting all the Ph.D.'s and giving them their instructions for the day. This was more European and structured than the lab I had been in while in Gothenburg, and it took me some time to learn what was going on.

    I started doing some work on a copper-containing protein, plastocyanin that is involved in photosynthesis. I was grasping at straws at this time because I really did not know that much about the field. Fortunately I sat next to David Knaff, who was a very smart biophysicist/biochemist who had recently come to the lab after getting his Ph.D. at Yale, and through these interactions, I at least came up with the an understanding of the basics of this complex system.

When we returned to Berkeley in the summer, Carole was pregnant again and our second son, Jesse Dylan, was born at the Kaiser Hospital in Oakland on November 2, 1969. Shortly after his birth, we bought an old, Berkeley craftsman style home in North Berkeley, about a mile and a half from the lab. When I walked in, I often met David as he was walking up Cedar Street reading the New York Times. (David was a tried and true New Yorker who could not live without the Times and bagels.) We would stop by the greenhouse to pick our hydroponically grown spinach leaves that were our prime scientific material and then go onto the lab to do our work for the day.

1967 El Dorado Avenue, Berkeley CA

I also started running around this time, and I got pretty serious about this activity. Starting slowly, I worked myself up to about 10 miles a day and decided that I should try some races. They were fairly short races at the beginning but I finally moved up to running marathons. There were so many of these in the Bay Area that you could pretty much run one a month if you were foolish enough. I was not bad at these and ultimately qualified for the Boston Marathon although for various reasons it turned out to be one of my worst efforts.

At this time, I also contacted Alan Bearden, whom I had met at the Gordon Conference. He was at the other end of the campus, but it was only a 10-minute walk to his lab. We decided to try and identify some of the first products of photosynthesis, that is, the stable chemical compounds that are formed after light is absorbed. We would use the same general biophysical instruments that I had used in the Swedish lab, so I was not totally lost. I provided the biological material for our work and Alan provided the instrumentation, including the computer technology that we required. I think each of us was very good at what we did and the output was more than $1+1 = 2$.

The Oakland Marathon with my helper, Jesse-1981

One thing that was obvious from the arrangement that Alan and I had was that it was independent of Professor Arnon. I informed him that I was collaborating with Alan and gave him a broad description of what were doing, but that was all. I did not realize this could have been trouble for me later, but fortunately for me, when we started doing our experiments they turned out very well. We almost immediately obtained some very significant results and these were submitted to the Proceedings of the National Academy of Sciences for publication. The paper was submitted by Professor Arnon (only members can submit papers) but his name was not on the paper as a co-author. I think this was the first time that a paper had come out of the lab without his name on it, but he could recognize the significance of the work, and it was still associated with the Department.

Alan and I collaborated on a wide range of investigations and our work was well received by the photosynthesis community. We were invited to give presentations at national and international meetings over the years, and this was important for me if I wanted to get a tenured faculty position at Berkeley. In 1979, my appointment was changed to that of an Associate Professor with tenure, which meant I could apply for my own research funding. The National Science Foundation funded my first grant proposal, based on the work I did with Alan, and this funding continued for the next 20 years. Funding was essential for supporting post-doctoral fellows and technical staff and during my career I had a series of postdocs who came into the lab and worked with me. I find it interesting that over this period, I continued to do my own research. As time moved on and I moved more into the academic world, my direct involvement decreased because of other obligations that are put upon faculty members, such as professional and campus service. We also started to teach regularly in the department, beginning with a graduate class in photosynthesis that was team-taught by several people, including David and myself. David and I also initiated a new upper division class on bioenergetics, and I had my first experience with Berkeley undergraduates in this class.

Working in the Hilgard Hall lab-1975

One of the wonderful things about being a professor was that you became a member of an international group of colleagues. Photosynthesis is a small field and one would see the same people on a yearly basis at meetings. Carole would always come with to the international meetings as the accompanying spouse and she often saw more of the surrounding environs since I had the obligation of attending talks. One of my happiest memories is getting invited to a meeting in Japan because this was a place I had always wanted to visit. The Japan trip was linked to a visit to China because of a visiting professor from Nanking who had visited the department. We spent several weeks seeing both countries and were treated like visiting royalty. We especially enjoyed trips to Britain and made a number of life-long friends as a result of these trips. But more on this later.

Life was pretty good for the Malkin family through the 1970s and into the 1980s. All of our children went to the Berkeley public schools, and these gave them a pretty good education in those days. When Daniel was about 8 years old and in middle school at Columbus School, he had an opportunity one day to pick out a musical instrument. He selected the cello because he said no one had wanted to play it. That was a choice that was to change not only his life but ours as well. We tried to find a cello teacher for him and this led us to the Berkeley cello community, a large group of players of all ages. I was lucky that my old research advisor, Jesse, played the cello and he recommended his instructor, Millie Rosner. Millie lived across the town in Elmwood and when Daniel started studying with her, we began the cello car pool, driving him and the cello back and forth. Millie was a very demanding instructor, maybe too much for a young student, and she suggested Daniel should study with a former student, Ethan Grumbach. Daniel and Ethan immediately hit it off. One thing that was unusual with Daniel was that we never had to tell him to practice. Once he started playing, he showed an enormous discipline and could play for hours. He worked hard and his musical talent showed. Neither Karin nor Jesse got into music, maybe because Daniel was so successful. As for Carole, she had completed her Antioch requirements shortly after I came to Berkeley as a graduate student, and as the children grew, she started writing and even went over to San Francisco State to get an M.A. degree in Creative Writing. For many years, she would come over to campus to write in my office on the 3rd floor of Hilgard Hall since she did not like writing at home. More on this later too.

In 1977, I had the opportunity to take a sabbatical leave. We decided to go to London for the year and I would work in the lab of Jim Barber at Imperial College. I had met Jim at a meeting in Holland in the early 1970s, and we immediately hit it off. I continued to see him at meetings, like the Gordon Conferences and international meetings, and it was always great fun so we thought it would be an exciting thing to be able to spend more time with him and his family and do a little science in London. We again were blessed with good luck when we sublet a three-story row house in St. John's Wood. St. John's Wood is, as the British would say, a very "posh" area. Karin and Jesse attended the local school, Barrows School, which was an intimidating building that looked like a cross between a prison and hospital. It was a 10-minute walk to school for them. Daniel's situation was more complicated. We could not get him into the Hampstead Secondary School (high school) but we found out about the Purcell School of Music in Harrow where he might go. The three of us had to be interviewed by the Headmaster and we all dressed up as well as we could and were very prim and proper and also successful in getting him admitted. In contrast to Karin and Jesse, Daniel had to take the "tube" to school, transfer trains, all the time carrying his cello with him every day. I should say finally that all the kids did wonderfully in their respective schools.

      I had picked up a Volvo station wagon when we arrived in London and this allowed us to drive around the city and also do some traveling. Driving in London was not fun because I had to make sure I was on the "right" side of the road. This became more of a problem if we left the city where there was much less traffic to follow. We did take three trips out to the countryside. The first was to Kent along the south coast and we were able to visit Canterbury and several coastal castles that the kids loved running around. The second was to the Cotswolds and Shakespeare country and the final trip in the spring before we left was to the Scottish border region. This last one was quite amusing because we could barely understand what the natives were saying even though we knew it was some kind of English.

Though I described our out of town trips, what made the year in London so special were all the wonderful things we did in the city. Daniel and I would take in musical events on the South Bank and at Wigmore Hall, and Carole and I went to the theater whenever we could. The Royal Shakespeare Company was still having a London season, and seeing and hearing Shakespeare's plays performed by the best in the world was exciting. The whole family would go off to the various museums and great buildings. Karin used to love to take the tube down to Trafalgar Square to feed the pigeons. It is hard to believe we let her go by herself but she was pretty independent in London. I remember she went off to the London zoo with her best friend, Kate, and they decided to see if they could get back home in a taxi. So they waved one down, had him bring them to our house, and then came in and asked me to pay the fare.

But the most special thing about our year was the friends we made: so many who turned out to be lifelong friends. Of course, there was the Barber family with Julie and Neil who were just about the same age as Karin and Jesse. Carole made some good friends from a literary class she took at Morley College. The class was taught by now Dame Margaret Drabble, a very distinguished English writer, who taught this class to mostly little old ladies who had been in it for years. But Carole met Nina Zucker who lived across the road from us and they hit it off and have stayed in touch for the next 30 years. But the greatest treasure of all was coming in contact with and getting to know the Elias family, a large group of Indian Jews. Carole made the contact because she was working on her grandfather's memoir (The Journeys of David Toback) published in 1981. The matriarch of the family was Flower, whom we grew to love over the years and told us after many years that we were not friends but family. We would go to Flower's flat every Monday evening for "Morag", a time of gathering of any family members who were around and everyone would eat an Indian dinner and spend time talking and/or arguing over the most current controversial topics. Her sister Mercia and her brother Arial were regular attendees as were her children and grandchildren. It was always like a 3-ring circus for us to be in the middle of what sometimes seemed like mayhem. But this was just the way of the Elias's. After we returned to Berkeley, Carole and Flower kept in contact by mail and anytime we returned to London after this first trip, we were always invited over for Monday "Morag."

    On a slightly different subject, shortly before we were to leave London, Carole took a package tour to the Soviet Union.

The tour went to Kiev, Leningrad and Moscow. Carole had been working for several years with a manuscript that her grandfather, David Toback, had written concerning his emigration to the USA. The long manuscript was written in Yiddish and Carole found someone who could translate it. She then was putting the memoir together in a novelistic style as David traveled across Europe to Antwerp where he left for New York. She wanted to see anything she could on he trip that related to David's trip. The most useful part of her trip was in Kiev where she visited an outdoor "museum" that contained examples of Russian peasant life. The book was submitted for publication in 1981 and published by Schocken Books, with the title "The Journeys of David Toback." It was a critical success with a major review in the Sunday Times Book Section. After publication, Carole went out on several book tours on the East and West Coasts. The only downside of her trip was that she had the "turista" in Leningrad and spent several days in a Russian hospital. In fact, the Russians wanted to quarantine her for several weeks but the tour guide was able to convince them that she was not contagious. It was an exciting experience that ended our exciting year abroad.

4. Berkeley-the 1980s: Health problems and academic politics

After returning to Berkeley in the summer of 1978, our life slipped back into normal routines. One thing of significance came about when Daniel told us he wanted to go to a conservatory after graduating from high school. His experience at the Purcell School was so positive that he knew he wanted to have music as his career. This was somewhat surprising to us but the cello had become his life long passion, and there was no doubt this was not simply a whim that would quickly pass. He began to investigate conservatories, emphasizing the cellists at each school since that would be the most important factor in his decision. Carole and Daniel went on a tour of music schools in spring 1980, and these included the Oberlin College Conservatory, Eastman School of Music and the New England Conservatory. After meeting with Lawrence Lesser at the New England Conservatory, Daniel decided this was his first choice and after being accepted, he looked forward to his new life in Boston. I remember so well when Carole and I took Daniel to the Oakland Airport to send him off to Boston. After we watched the plane take off, we went into the airport restaurant and both of us just cried. Daniel was our first child and had grown to be a sensitive, caring young man. We knew that once he left home, his connection to us would not be the same.

    Professionally, the 1980s were busy for me. I had received a second research grant from the National Institutes of Health in the early 1980s, and I was pleased to have been successful because it meant that I had convinced the NIH of the relevance of my work in plants for the "health of the American public." Long-term support was secure and I could bring in people to work without worrying where the money was going to come from. We were making good progress in a number of research areas during this time.

Los Angeles Olympic Games-1984

In the mid-1980s, 1985 to be exact, our peace and quiet was shocked. Carole went into Kaiser in Oakland for a checkup after finding a lump in one of her breasts. Carole's mother had died in her early 40s and she lived with a fear of breast cancer as she grew up and into adult hood. A surgeon removed the small lump and assured her that "It was nothing." A week later she went to see him again to get the biopsy report and she was told she had breast cancer. I did not accompany her to the doctor that time because of his early certainty about the lump and I still remember getting a phone call from her while at work telling me it was cancer. Treatment decisions had to be made quickly and Carole and I agreed that she should have a double mastectomy to decrease the possibility of any future problems even though there was no spread to any lymph nodes. It was an enormously brave decision on her part. She had surgery at Kaiser and made a good recovery and we believed this this procedure would end the breast cancer threat.

While we thought Carole was safe and got on with our lives, the next four years were filled with trauma. Carole had four small cancerous nodules removed and also was treated with radiation therapy and finally chemotherapy to try to stop these cancers from recurring. After the final chemotherapy treatment, she was in apparent remission. This turned out not to be true since Carole had a small cancerous nodule along her mastectomy scar in 1989 and another in 1990. These were treated with standard chemotherapy and this appeared to be effective because the nodule disappeared. It was clear from these localized recurrences that Carole's cancer was behaving in an unusual manner since all of these recurrences occurred in the same region and there was no evidence for metastasis. The chemotherapy was pretty rough on her with the common side effects, but she came through it all.

      Unfortunately our medical problems were not yet over. After Daniel had gotten his undergraduate degree at the New England Conservatory, he moved to Baltimore to obtain an artist's diploma (equivalent to a Master's degree) at the Peabody Conservatory of Music, studying with an Israeli cellist, Yehuda Hanani.

      Daniel had noticed he had a medium size mole on his back, but he did not do anything about it for some time. In the mid 1980s, he found it was getting larger, and he finally went to a dermatologist who did a biopsy and reported that it was a melanoma. Treatment for melanoma was limited to surgery in those days and the melanoma was removed but it was found to be a Stage III melanoma, which is very serious. He was told to keep his eyes on it and hope for the best. During this time, Daniel had met a Korean violinist, Wonju Kim, also at Peabody and their relationship became serious and they decided to get married. It had been almost five years since the melanoma was removed, and we all felt that the problem was done with and he was in remission. Their marriage in 1989 was a grand Korean-American combination event with Wonju's large family coming all the way from Seoul for the event. Both Wonju and Daniel were fortunate to obtain symphony positions in the Washington/Baltimore area. Daniel was playing with the Kennedy Center Orchestra/Washington National Opera Orchestra and Wonju with the Baltimore Symphony. To accommodate both of them, they were living in Columbia, MD, midway between the two cities.

My academic life became more complicated in the 1980s. I was asked to be on a National Science Foundation review panel that dealt with proposals on biophysical and biochemical aspects of photosynthesis and was happy to serve although it meant many trips to Washington and many proposals to read and evaluate. I was also selected by my peers to be the Chairman for the Photosynthesis Gordon Conference in 1987, and it was a great honor and also a lot of work. Things at the University were even more complicated. Professor Arnon, the chairman of Cell Physiology, retired in the early 1980s, and the administration decided the department was too small to remain as an independent academic unit. A new unit, the Division of Molecular Plant Biology, was established in 1985 with Bob Buchanan as the chair. We were associated with the Department of Plant Pathology at that time. I followed Bob as chair in 1988, but at that time bigger changes were about to occur.

In the mid-1980s, the campus initiated a review of the biological sciences. Many department names, such as Physiology-Anatomy, were considered dated and academic appointments were not in tune with recent developments that had shown biology was becoming a more molecular science. In the case of plant biology, there were three academic units that had plant-related faculty: Botany, Genetics and Molecular Plant Biology. In addition, the major biological science buildings were badly out-of date. The way the campus deals with a situation like this is, of course, to form a committee to evaluate current programs and give direction to new programs. Also, the committee should identify new physical structures where they are needed. My own personal problem was that I was pretty knowledgeable about the plant sciences on campus and I was pretty honest about strengths and weaknesses. So I was appointed to the Chancellor's Advisory Council of Biology. The recommendations of this group covered all areas of biology, but I need only tell you what was recommended for plant sciences: a new department of plant biology that would emphasize molecular, biochemical and physiological plant biology, with faculty from the above three departments. And it was suggested that I become the first chairman of the department because I was the only person who got along with almost the entire faculty in the new department. In addition the campus raised money for the construction a new building, the Genetics and Plant Biology

Building that would house the new department. There is some irony in that this new building was to be located next to the Biochemistry Building, the very place where I had gotten my Ph.D. with Jesse.

The reorganization and the move of some 20 faculty into new space took several years, and for me personally, these were difficult times. I felt very much like a therapist as I had to deal with a multitude of academic problems, such as setting up new graduate and undergraduate programs, and a multitude of problems relating to getting people settled into their new space. All I can say is that I did the best job I could and tried to treat everyone fairly although it was stressful. I learned quite a bit about Berkeley faculty and became rather cynical about many of them for their selfishness and often pettiness. In addition to dealing with my own faculty, I also had to interact with some of the academic administrators on the campus, and this often resulted in frustration as the administration dealt with its own priorities. My conclusion at the end of a four-year term as department chair was that I had just completed the most difficult job at the university.

The 1980s ended on a very positive note. Both Karin and Jesse went off to college in the 1980s with Karin attending Barnard in 1986 and Jesse Oberlin in 1987. In addition to Daniel's wedding, Karin was married the summer of 1989. Karin had become seriously Orthodox in her teen-age years and actually finished high school in Skokie, IL where she attended a Jewish school. She met Ari Blumofe at that time and continued to see him when she was in New York at Barnard. All this culminated in their marriage in a very Jewish wedding in Skokie. Karin had decided to go to medical school and she started at the University of Southern California shortly after receiving her BA degree. Jesse's career took a different turn when he was selected as a Rhodes Scholar and was able to spend two years in studies at Oxford University. After returning from England, Jesse received a Ph.D. degree in health economics from the Rand Graduate School in Santa Monica. In 1993, he married Michelle Maglalang whom he had met at Oberlin.

  During the 1970s and 1980s, I was fortunate to be invited to a large number of scientific meetings. Whenever possible, Carole would come along as the "accompanying spouse," and she would be entertained at local sites while I was doing my science. Travel to foreign countries also occurred and most of these trips were to Western Europe. We went to Reading, Halkidiki, Greece, and Brussels. The Greek trip was special because we took a bus tour from Athens up to the north and saw much of the Greek landscape. There was also a trip to Prague thrown in for a Biophysics congress and we were lucky to have Jim Barber there for the meeting as well.

Nanjing, China-1985

I always wanted to go to the Far East, particularly Japan, but that opportunity had not come up. In early 1985, I remember receiving a letter from Kei Wada, a Japanese scientist who had spent two years in the Department of Cell Physiology. He returned to a position at Osaka University and was writing to invite me to a symposium on iron-sulfur proteins, the very subject I was studying in my lab. That afternoon, I carried this letter home and came into our house and said to Carole, "I have gotten something I always wanted." I am not sure what she thought was going on until I told her I had an invitation to go to Japan. We made this trip in fall of 1985 and connected it to a trip to China because a Chinese scientist from Nanjing had also been in the lab at the same time and was able to invite Carole and myself to come to China. This was the trip of our life. We flew from San Francisco to Hong Kong and then went on to Shanghai, Nanjing and Beijing. In China we were treated like visiting royalty, meeting Presidents of universities and being taken around to see all the most important sites. From China, we flew to Osaka and spent time in Tokyo and Kyoto as well. The visit to Kyoto was most special because it was "Old Japan," which meant it had not been destroyed during World War II and had retained the beauty of Japan with its wondrous temples. Being there in the fall was even more special because of the changing of the colors in the trees that were on the mountains surrounding the city. I had the opportunity to go back to Japan several times after this first trip and visited Kei Wada several times in Kanazawa where he became a Professor.

5. Berkeley-the 1990s: Teaching and More Health Problems

The 1990s did not start well as my mother died on March 15, 1991. After my father died, she had left Chicago and moved to Los Angeles and then Escondido to live with her older sister, Rose. After a number of years, she met Morris Mandell, a widower who had come to the West Coast from Detroit. After several years, they married and Morris became part of our family. He was a very kind man and enjoyed coming up to Berkeley to visit and tried to fix just about everything in our old Berkeley home, with little success. Morris died in the late 1980s and Lorry and I convinced my mom to move up to the Bay area to be near us. She lived in several retirement places for a number of years and finally moved to Santa Rosa where Lorry was living. Her health started to deteriorate in 1990 as she had dementia and finally a stroke. She died a year later. She asked to be buried in Chicago in the grave cemetery with my father, at a site where other Malkin family members were buried and we all met there for a short memorial service. I did not feel her loss very much as we were not close for so many years but it was still sad to think about the passing of that generation forever.

    As part of the reorganization within biology that had occurred earlier, a faculty committee considered the basic entry course for all biology majors. The course, Biology 1A and 1B, was one of the largest classes on the campus, with each class enrolling well over 1000 students each semester. Campus administrators were aware that these enrollments were so large that the instruction in the class was becoming less effective. The proposed solution to this problem was to offer Biology 1A and Biology 1B each semester instead of once per year. Personally, I was quite amused by this decision since going from a class with 1000 students to a class with 500 students did not seem to offer much change for the students in these courses. Since each class is team-taught by 3 instructors, it would also require 6 new faculty for instruction. It was my impression from being on the campus for almost 20 years at that time that the pool of possible instructors was small, but as chairman of a department that was involved with instruction in both Biology 1A and 1B, it was my job to identify instructors. In the case of Biology 1A, it was rather easy because I wanted to teach in the course.

    My first time in the class was the last time of the old arrangement and we had over 1200 students. There is no class room on the Berkeley campus that can hold 1200 students so the "live" lecture was given at 8 am and the lecture was video-taped and shown at 11 am for students who did not make it to the 8AM lecture. When the new format was used in my second year, we had a class with about 440 students and no videotaping. I continued to teach in Biology 1A until I retired in 2012 and found it to be one of the most rewarding academic activities I had at Berkeley. Undergraduate students at Berkeley are bright and the ones we had were enthusiastic about the subject. I lectured on the structure and function of biological molecules and drew on examples that came from my own research interest in the general field of bioenergetics. The class was challenging to teach, and I learned the best I could do would come from my enthusiasm for the subject. I honestly believe that biology had emerged in the latter part of the 20th century the most exciting of the basic sciences and with the molecular revolution starting to take place, the best was yet to come. It was sometimes difficult to get this point across to a class that was had approximately 80% of students wanting to go to medical school, but that did not stop me from trying. I also took pride in probably being the only department chair teaching in such a basic course. People would ask me why I like teaching such a big class, and I would reply, "Because it's fun."

In the early 1990s, Carole's oncologist at Kaiser, Dr. Russell Staples, recommended that she should consider a relatively new treatment for breast cancer: high dose chemotherapy treatment. This recommendation came after another nodule was present in the same chest region. The treatment had been shown in several medical centers, most notably Duke, to be more effective than standard chemotherapy as a treatment for breast cancer. It involved a dose of chemotherapy drugs, with thirty-times the amount used for normal chemotherapy. It also required an autologous bone marrow transplant where the bone marrow was removed prior to treatment and then given back to the patient after the chemotherapy regime. The procedure involved a 6-8 week hospitalization in an isolation ward because of the total destruction of all white blood cells by the high dose chemotherapy drugs and the increased the risk of infection. However, after we received this recommendation, Kaiser refused to do the procedure, arguing it was an experimental treatment. We moved Carole's medical care to UCSF with Dr. Lloyd Damen in the Hematology-Oncology Unit, and he supervised the procedure at UCSF. We also starting seeing Dr. Debu Tripathy, a young breast cancer specialist, who continued to take an active role in Carole's cancer management.

The procedure turned out to be as horrible as advertised, and Carole was sick and weak for over six weeks before her white blood cell count finally started to return to normal. I drove over to UCSF every morning and gave what help I could. I would get her out of bed every morning and we would walk around the ward, over and over, to build up her strength. Everyone on the ward recognized us as the constant walkers. Finally, she was able to show Dr. Damon she could take in some food and was allowed to go home. There are so many other stories I could tell about this entire experience, but I will warn you at this time that this story is not over.

In 1992, I stepped down as chairman of the Department of Plant Biology. I felt I had done a good job in that the department had come up with new curricula for graduate and undergraduate students and much of the friction among the faculty seemed under control. There was a major redistribution of financial resources that resulted in everyone obtaining some internal funding for their individual research projects. The amount of money was not substantial but it was more equally distributed. And our staff members had learned how to deal with a diverse group of faculty, some of whom could be pretty nasty. So I could retire from this position knowing that I was the first chairman of the Department of Plant Biology, for whatever that is worth.

London-Jim Barber's Office-1994

I did not return to regular academic years after quitting the chairman job. Instead, Dean Will Gardner of the College of Natural Resources asked me if I would become the Associate Dean for Academic Affairs in the Dean's Office. I knew Will well, having worked closely with him on the biology reorganization, and the opportunity to be associated with him and his staff in the Dean's Office was attractive. It also took me out of the departmental politics that were occurring in my own department. The position had many critical functions in the

College: the appointment of new faculty, the review of all faculty academic actions, such as merit raise increases and promotions. Since I did many of these things at the departmental level, I felt I could easily step into this job. I thought it would be a position I would hold for 4-5 years but I ended up holding the position for over 10 years. I also became the Program Manager for the USDA grant program in photosynthesis for 1992-1993, and this involved spending a fair amount of time in Washington, D.C. for grant reviews and making decisions on funding.

I was not heavily involved in research during the 1990s and turned much of the responsibility to post-doctoral fellows in my lab. This was a conscious decision on my part and reflected my belief that retirement was not far off for me. I did not stop teaching my part of Biology 1A because the more I was involved in the course, the more I was enjoying it. I had another sabbatical coming up and applied for a Guggenheim Fellowship and was a little surprised that I was awarded a fellowship to return to London and spend my year working in Jim Barber's lab. Unfortunately this trip never came off as Carole had another breast cancer scare about a month before we planned to go to London and we decided we should not leave Berkeley at that time. I contacted the Guggenheim Foundation and asked if I could take my fellowship in residence at Berkeley and they generously agreed so that I at least had some time off from my normal academic activities.

Carole's breast cancer situation continued to be a problem in the 1990s. After having the high dose chemotherapy procedure, we anticipated no more problems but seven months after the procedure she discovered another small tumor in the same region as the others and it was a cancerous growth. Clearly the high dose chemotherapy had not worked and some other treatment would have to be considered. While she had radiation when she was initially diagnosed, we thought more radiation was not an option. But the doctors at UCSF informed us that there were advances in radiation that made a second radiation treatment possible, and this is what she did. She was to have 25 treatments, but the side effects of shoulder and chest pain became too much, and she stopped after 23 treatments. Thus usual side effect of fatigue also increased as the treatments went on. Routine examinations over a period of 6-9 months showed no additional recurrences and after the one-year date of the radiation, it appeared that Carole had gone into remission. To jump further ahead and finish this point, there were no more breast cancer issues following this second radiation and after 5 years, her Berkeley oncologist told her to stop coming to see him, which was the best news we had had in almost 10 years.

With Jim Barber at UCLA-1996

In 1995, I took one of my most unusual foreign trips on behalf of our College. Professor Vince Resh, a good friend, and myself were invited to go to Russia and visit their science city, Puschino, where we were to discuss the Russian attempts to build academic programs more like those in the USA. Our trip was scheduled for November, which is certainly not a favorite time to visit Russia. Puschino is a stark, colorless city, which had many high-rise apartment buildings, built in the functional Russian style. Vince is an entomologist/ecologist and visited scientists in his area, while I visited mostly biophysicists and biochemists. When we went to Russia, the economy had pretty much collapsed and it was a very depressing place to be, and the people were struggling. We did have one weekend in Moscow where we were on our own and struggled to get around the city to see the major tourist sites, such as Red Square. What was so striking was seeing people at the subway exits standing on the streets selling household goods, such as cups and saucers, so they would have money for food. However, the food stores had little in them: a few potatoes and cabbages. This was not a fun trip and we came back feeling that the Russians were never going to achieve any kind of restructuring unless they could obtain the support of the government for this major overhaul.

Vince Resh and Dick, Moscow-1995

Unfortunately, health problems continued to plague us for the latter part of the 1990s. In this case, it was not Carole, but Daniel. In 1995, Daniel started to feel poorly, with hip pain that became worse with time. He saw a physical therapist, a chiropractor and even his regular family doctor, but no one came up with anything definite in terms of a diagnosis. He finally went to see his oncologist, who recommended an MRI scan, and the results were staggering. His melanoma had recurred and had spread to his bones and to several organs as well. When Carole and I were told this, we were devastated and having him some 3000 miles away made it all the more difficult. Daniel started to see a melanoma specialist at the Johns Hopkins Medical School, but the prognosis was not good. They had had their first child and our first grandchild, Abigail, in 1994 and Wonju was pregnant again when the diagnosis of melanoma came in. The doctor told Daniel that he hoped he could survive to see his next child born, which was expected to be in July 1996. Daniel started treatment immediately and initially had to have a hip replacement operation because the cancer had seriously weakened one hip. He then followed this with chemotherapy although he was told that the success rate with chemotherapy in the case of melanoma was extremely low. The drugs were hard on him and he needed lots of pain medications. We did what we could by shuttling between Berkeley and Columbia. For example,

I would drive Daniel to the cancer center for his chemotherapy treatments. It was a difficult time for all of us.

Sometimes in the midst of great pain and suffering, a ray of light emerges. When Daniel was having his treatments at Johns Hopkins, he met a young woman who also had Stage IV melanoma. Her name was Eva Cassidy and she lived with her parents in Bowie, MD, not far from Columbia. Eva was the same age as Daniel and was a pop singer in the Baltimore/Washington area. They would see each other at their over-lapping appointments and would mostly talk about their cancer situation. I met her at one treatment as well and in addition met her parents, Barbara and Hugh Cassidy. Eva passed away about five months before Daniel, on November 2, 1996, and after her death several recordings were made from tapes of her singing. These first CDs became smash hits and more were put out. Carole and I became close friends with Eva's parents over the years, and we were bonded together by what had happened to both of our children.

Daniel's treatments continued at Hopkins but the results were not good. We then contacted Dr. Steven Rosenberg at the National Institutes of Health. Dr. Rosenberg was recognized as one of the leading cancer investigators in the world and had been using interferon in experimental protocols on melanoma patients. For us, it was a last effort in our attempts to at least slow down the melanoma. We knew the side reactions of these experimental treatments could be serious, and this turned out to be the case with Daniel. He was a patient in-house at NIH and he had a bad reaction to the treatment. It was so bad that he had to go into the intensive care unit to be monitored 24 hours a day. When Daniel returned home, he was very weak and never truly recovered any strength. Carole and I felt the NIH experiment probably hastened his death.

    Daniel's second child, Ilana, was born on July 31, 1996 and for Daniel it was almost a miracle that he was there for the birth. He had little time with her and she does not have any memories of him. In the spring of 1997, he was still being cared for at home in Columbia. We were spending more time there, as his condition got worse. We did go home in early April, but shortly after, we received a call from Wonju that we should return. When we arrived in Columbia, we tried to convince Wonju that Daniel should enter the local hospice program, but she would not agree because she still believed he would get better. This turned out not to be true and he passed away in the early morning on April 24, 1997 at the Howard County General Hospital. Carole and I were both with him when he died, but he was never awake during this time because of the heavy pain medications he was given. I cannot describe in any way the feelings we both had as we looked over him as he passed on.

    There was much to take care of after Daniel died. We had made arrangements with a local funeral home for his cremation since this is what he requested. Carole decided she should be with Wonju and I remained in the hospital waiting the funeral home personnel to come. It was the saddest thing I have ever done: sitting in the hospital room with my son after he died waiting for several hours. After the cremation, Carole and I drove out to the funeral home to pick up the ashes, not knowing what we would do with them. I had discussed with Wonju about visiting local cemeteries, but she would not go. Finally, we had to return home to Berkeley and I told her we were taking the ashes with us. We made arrangements at a local cemetery, Sunset View Cemetery, which was only 10 minutes away from our house and Daniel's ashes are buried there. We also purchased the plot next to Daniel's for future use.

    I have never felt like I did when we returned to Berkeley after Daniel's death. The everyday things of life felt trivial and the sadness was overwhelming. Both Carole and I struggled through the days but for me, I could not stop asking one question: Why did this happen? How can it be that a child dies before their parent? This is not the way of nature. We would go to the cemetery often and both of us would talk to Daniel, seeking some kind of answers that we knew we would never get. There were a few close friends who tried to help us but there was little solace. Then there were the "friends" who avoided us like the plague, running across the street so they would not have to talk with us or turning away when they saw us coming. Would it have taken so much of them to simply acknowledge our loss with a simple, "So sorry about your loss?" I learned during this time that one has "fair-weather-friends" who are not willing to be there when they are really needed.

At some point I had to return to work and reactions were the same in that most of my colleagues in my department did not even acknowledge what had happened to Carole and myself. The staff of the Dean's Office was much more kind and understanding. It was just about impossible to get back to work. I was in a fog most of the time and could not focus and on what seemed like petty details in the academic world.

After several months, we looked for a grief group to help us through this period of mourning. Some were what I call "touchy-feely" groups that were of no value to us. We finally found a group, associated with the Visiting Nurses Association in Emeryville, that was led by Daniel Potaphshyn, that helped us, and we were both indebted to him for his support and care. One thing we learned was that one does not get through grief quickly and that in a situation of great loss, such as the loss of a child, it goes on and on. It changes in the way you react but it is still present years after the loss. On several occasions, Carole would dream about Daniel and talk with him in those dreams. Assuming that I do dream, I rarely remember dreams and never had a dream with Daniel in it. He used to call us early in the morning when he knew we were up and about, and I still recall the sound of his voice in these conversations.

One thing we vowed to do: maintain a close contact with our two granddaughters. They were very small when Daniel died and neither remembers much of him. We wanted them to know him as they grew up and to know how wonderful a man he was as well as appreciate how wonderful a father he would have been. This we would do by talking to them often, telling them stories about him. When we started out weekly phone calls, Abby was about two and a half and Ilana only 18 months. We have continued these calls all the way up to now, with both girls being in college. If I do not call them on the weekend, they call me and we have the warmest and loving relationship with each of them. The situation got more complicated when Wonju remarried a man with 3 of his own children, and we have tried to maintain a good relationship with these three stepchildren as well as the new stepfather but it has been difficult over the years.

The remainder of the 1990s went along as we tried to adjust to the terrible events that came earlier. I continued to struggle through my academic affairs, including teaching in Biology 1A. One high point of this time was that I received the Distinguished Teaching Award from the college in 1999. It was nice to know that my teaching efforts even though I was an Associate Dean were being recognized.

6. Berkeley-2000 and on: moving toward retirement

By the end of the 1990s, we had three granddaughters because Karin's first child, Talia, was born in 1997. Over the next several years, we had two more granddaughters, Maia in Karin's family, and Veronica, in Jesse's family. At this point I felt I could manage a Malkin family girl's basketball team. This all changed in 2002 and 2003 when Karin's son, Adin, was born and Jesse's son, Julian, was born. With seven grandchildren spread over three different cities (Karin was living in Chicago at the time and Jesse was in the Baltimore area), we spent a great deal of time flying across the country to visit as many kids as we could.

The year 2000 did not start well for us. On January 27th, my brother, Lorry, died after suffering a long, slow illness with lung disease. He had moved back to Aptos, CA, after living many years in Avon, CO. He moved to Colorado because of his passion for skiing, but when his lung capacity started to diminish, doctors told him the altitude was only making it worse. They were never able to tell him what was causing this illness. We saw him often in Aptos and after years of not feeling close to each other, there was some kind of emotional reconciliation and we enjoyed going down to his home and visiting. During this time, we also became much closer to two of my nieces, Julie, the older one, and Jamie, the younger one. After my brother died, he wanted part of his ashes spread on the Colorado ski slopes, some on San Francisco Bay and the remainder on our parents' grave in Chicago. Carole and I went on the bay trip and also to Chicago. In some ways he became a role model for me because in the last 15 or so years of his life, he did wanted he wanted to do and that was ski. One day we were talking on the phone and the subject of retirement came up because I told him I was considering retiring. He asked me two questions: Do you still like your job and do you need the money. My answer to the first part was that I didn't like it as much as I used to, and to the second part that I did not need the money. So, he concluded, I should really think about retiring.

I spent more time in the Dean's Office in the early 2000s working to establish teaching as a high priority for our faculty. In a time when resources were becoming more limited because of decreased funding from the state, I felt that the College had to attract more students and improve its teaching programs. My message was simple: the faculty had to become more involved in teaching undergraduates. This was a big challenge for me to convince faculty of the increasing importance of undergraduate education and the only clout I could bring to the table was to inform them that when they were evaluated for a merit increase or a promotion, I would seriously look at their undergraduate teaching record. As long as Berkeley faculty believed that the only important area for advancement was research, it would be hard to convince anyone that their teaching function was also critical. I am not sure I made much progress but some departments were showing increasing enrollments as they strived to improve their programs.

As I started to think about more seriously about retirement, I also let people in my lab know that they should start to look for other positions. My lab was still supported with funding from both NIH and NSF, but I was somewhat detached from the actual research going on in the lab and I told my several postdocs that they were free to publish by themselves if they wished. It seemed to me that more papers with my name on them just was not that important any more. My NSF grant would be up for renewal in 2003, and my decision was to not try to get the grant renewed. The same would hold for my NIH grant in 2004 so that my research activities would stop after 2004.

Although I had been an Associate Dean for a number of years, I was asked by the Chancellor to assume the position of Acting Dean of the College for three years, starting in 2000. This came about because an attempt to hire a new Dean was not successful and they needed someone to step up and take over for this interim period. It was not a job I particularly wanted to do

Lecturing in Japan-2003

because one of the things you had to do was to try and raise money for the College's programs. I did meet a fair number of people in the private sector who were either alumni or were associated with the College in some way and many of these people had gone on to interesting professions. One individual, Rocky Main, had been at Berkeley in the early 1940s and married a forestry student who went on to open a sawmill in Northern California. Unfortunately, he died fairly young, leaving her with five sons. When I first met her, I felt strongly that Carole would like her very much and I arranged for the two of them to sit next to each other at some College function. I was totally on the right track as we all became good friends and although she lived in Redding CA up north, she came to Berkeley often for events and would stay with us on these trips. We even took a couple of drives up to Redding, CA to visit with her in her home. I guess Rocky was some kind of mother figure for both Carole and myself, and it was wonderful to get to know her and I guess I have to acknowledge that I would not have met her if I had not been Dean. Unfortunately for us, Rocky passed away on December 22, 2005, and we lost someone who meant so very much to both of us.

In the middle 2000s, Carole started to have another health problem. She was having low back pain and it finally was diagnosed as spinal stenosis/sciatica. As with this syndrome, the pain could be quite intense and she was having trouble walking any kind of distance. For a while she was trying yoga, Pilates, etc. and then went on to physical therapy and steroid injections. In the spring of 2004, the American Society of Plant Biologists notified me that I had been awarded the Kettering Award in Photosynthesis. Besides being completely surprised at this, I was also very happy to receive it because it is probably the most significant award in the field (other than a Nobel Prize but I was certainly not in that category). I bring this up now because I was to go to Orlando Florida to receive the award during the summer. Carole and I went out to Florida in August and the weather was pretty unbearable for us: hot and humid. Carole could not get around very well and we needed a wheelchair for her. It was actually pretty sad for both of us because of her health. When we returned to Berkeley, it was time to see a surgeon and again, as we had in the past, we turned to our friend Marshall to find out who was good at UCSF. He told us the only back surgeon he would trust was Dr. Philip Weinstein, a neurosurgeon whom he knew very well. After a difficult time trying to get an appointment, we met with him after Carole had several scans of her lower back and he recommended she have a laminectomy, a procedure that enlarges the spinal canal so that pressure on the nerves is relieved. Her problem came from arthritis in the spinal region. On October 4, 2012, Carole went into the hospital at UCSF for her surgery. And on October 4, 2012, I officially retired from UC Berkeley.

When I retired, I closed down my lab and gave up my laboratory space. I did retain my office because I had decided to continue to teach in Biology 1A. I thought I would just do this for a few years, but it turned out to be an 8-year job, running through the fall of 2012. I also made the decision not to ask for any payment and that I would donate my services to UC Berkeley. I never actually calculated how much money the University was saving by not paying me, but I thought this was a donation to the University and that they were getting a pretty good deal because I did a really good job in this class and enjoyed it even more in my retirement. Students would ask me if they could work in my lab at this time and I told them I was retired, which they were very surprised to hear. "So why are you still teaching in Biology 1A?" was a common response from them. To which I would reply, "Because I really enjoy the students in this class."

Carole's recovery after her surgery was slow and steady. The doctor gave her all kinds of specific instructions about what she could and could not do, all relating to not twisting or turning her back. And she was told not to pick up anything, which she took very seriously. The first day we went out after getting home, we walked from our house to the corner, turned around and went home. The next day she wanted to go further, but I insisted we do the same short walk. It went like this for about a month, but she gradually regained her strength and, more importantly, she was pain free. Many days we would say to each other, "Thank God for Dr. Weinstein," and we meant it.

In 2004, there were several events related to my retirement. One was a large College-wide reception attended mostly by staff and faculty with a smattering of students too. People gave very warm thanks to me for all the efforts I had made in the College. I actually received a number of nice gifts from individuals as well. It was held outside in the courtyard of one of our buildings on a nice Spring afternoon, and I felt pleased that maybe I had made a little difference in the lives of some over the 35 years that I was a faculty member and administrator. This was followed by the last commencement a few weeks later and to my surprise I was given the Berkeley Citation. This award was given to distinguished faculty upon their retirement if they had made substantial contributions to the campus over the course of their careers. It was not given out automatically when you retired and I felt very honored to receive it although it was to be given by Chancellor Robert Berdahl, but he was called away at the last minute so that the Dean of our College gave it to me. To be perfectly honest, I think I deserved this award after spending so much of my time working both as a regular faculty member and also as an administrator at all levels over my career.

After retiring, my life became much more relaxed. Even though I continued to teach, my time was my own and I did what I wanted to do when I wanted to do it. There were no more meetings or other academic affairs that I had to go to. Some faculty continued to participate in departmental meetings after they retired, but it seemed that one's colleague and campus authorities essentially put you out to pasture the day that you retired and you were not called upon to do much of anything. I did become involved with the campus Emeriti Association because I thought this could be an important group to lobby for emeriti matters. In fact, I ended up being President of the Association for three years even though I was told it was a one-year position. It turned out to be a critical time for emeriti as the campus administration tried to change the campus rules for emeriti parking (proposing a substantial increase in fees for emeriti), but I like to think that I spear-headed a movement to leave us alone, and we won the battle. It was not often the administration gave in on a topic like this.

Angel's Landing, Zion National Park, October 2008

The only ripple in a somewhat quiet pond came about in 2009. Carole and I had been having dermatology appointments twice a year because of the problems of melanoma in our family. Fortunately for us, our dermatologist, Dr. Kathy Fang, was not only an excellent doctor but she became a good friend. On one visit, Kathy saw something on Carole's scalp and decided to do a biopsy of it. I remember that is was a Friday night and she called us at home to tell us she had just gotten the pathology report and it was melanoma. She lived close to us and said she was immediately coming over to talk with us about this result. We did not cry at the news because I think we were in a state of shock when we received this result from Kathy. This was so different from when Carole was told about her breast cancer because that was totally unexpected. Our reactions were muted because, I think, we could not believe this was happening to us again. After Kathy left, I held her and we talked. I told her she had gotten through the breast cancer and she would get through this. I believed this with all my heart.

About ten minutes later, she was at our door and we talked about what to do next. She knew several doctors in the Melanoma Clinic at UCSF and recommended we see Dr. M. Kashani as soon as possible. I think our first appointment with him was the next week and she had sent him the pathology report. The melanoma was stage I, which was a relief, but it had to be completely removed surgically. He recommended Dr. Wang, who was a UCSF neck and head surgeon working with cancer patients. A surgical appointment was scheduled and Dr. Wang not only did the excision but also did what is called a sentinel node biopsy to test for whether there was any spread of the melanoma from the primary site. The results were the best we could have gotten as Dr. Wang reported that there were clear margins at the site and the biopsy was negative. The doctors were all positive and this is what we wanted to hear. If we needed a result that would make us celebrate, this was about as good as it gets in the cancer business.

Yellowstone National Park, June 2010

After this scare in 2009, we believed we had caught the melanoma in an early stage and the evidence that there was no spread to the lymphatic system was an indication it had not spread beyond that site. Still, Carole and I decided that she should have regular dermatology appointments with both Dr.

Fang and Dr. Kashani so she had two visits a year, one with each doctor. However, at the same time, we started to seriously think about moving nearer to one of our two children. We had several older friends who were living far from family members and this led to complications when a serious health issue came up. Of course, we had our own experience with Daniel's illness and him living across the country. Jesse and his family had moved to Colorado Springs in July 2008 and for various reasons we thought this might be the place to move to if and when we made the decision. We had visited them several times, but they had not settled into a home for two years after their move, and it would have been premature to finalize anything.

In 2010, we were looking forward to our 50th wedding anniversary on Christmas Day. Abby and Ilana came out to California and Jesse and his family were with us, so we had enough people for a nice family gathering at home. It was not a big deal since we are not into parties very much, but I did get a rather elegant special cake from our local bakery, The Virginia Bakery, since we had been going there since Daniel was a little boy. The day after Christmas Jesse insisted that we all go out to dinner and he wanted to go somewhere fancy so he had picked a place in Oakland that we had eaten at once and I told him it wasn't special, but he said he had been told by someone that it was great, and he wanted to go there. Around dinner time we all piled into our cars and drove over to the restaurant in a torrential rain storm, and when we got there, the hostess said she had a special "room" for such a large group. We followed her around and finally got to this place and when I walked in, the first person I saw standing there was Karin. I looked around and realized all of our family and Berkeley friends were there and that it was a surprise 50th anniversary party. We were totally fooled by the whole thing and I never thought something like this would happen. It was great for us to see all these people and, of course, there were toasts and speeches from the invited guests. All in all, a wonderful evening set up by both Karin and Jesse for us.

Part III. On to Colorado-2012

Colorado Springs home-2012

Jesse and Michelle bought a house in Colorado Springs in 2010 and this led us to consider moving. I was still teaching in Biology 1A but I was also thinking that it was time to step down. I had taught in the class for almost 20 years and it was probably the most rewarding time I had at Berkeley. It would be a major undertaking to leave Berkeley after over 40 years. But we started to look at homes when we went to visit him and finally found a house. After much negotiation in the Fall of 2011, we purchased our new home. However, we still were living in Berkeley, trying to decide what to do with our El Dorado home. I first thought we would keep the El Dorado house, rent it out and possible spend the winter months in California. The more I toyed with that plan, the less I liked it, and we finally contacted a realtor about selling in the spring of 2012. We turned our attention to getting the house for sale and worked like dogs cleaning, clearing, etc. In May 2012, the house was empty and ready to go on the market and we climbed in our car and drove off to Colorado Springs

    It was strange leaving Berkeley after so many years and so many memories. It did not affect me much when we were packing and clearing up the house, but when the house was totally empty, I walked around all of the rooms and thought about all that we had been through in that home. I call it our home because this was the only house I had ever lived in, it was the place where we raised our three children and saw them grow up and leave and take on their own lives. Each room was filled with so many memories, particularly Daniel's room with the pitting of the floor from the end pin of his cello. It was sad to leave this place where there were so many joyful memories and also the memories of such sadness at our trials and tribulations. But we knew we were doing the right thing as we climbed into our Honda and headed off.

    Driving to Colorado from California is not what I would call fun. Northern Nevada and Utah are pretty boring unless you like desert-like areas. But we made it safely and a few days after our arrival, a moving van appeared with 75 boxes that needed emptying. So we had plenty of work ahead of us, but we were in no rush and settled into a rather simple life in Colorado. All of this changed several weeks later. It was a Saturday and we had gone out to do some shopping when, upon leaving the store around noon, we noticed smoke on the mountains to the west. I asked someone what was going on and they said there was a fire in Waldo Canyon. I had no idea exactly where that was but I thought it was near where we were living. I immediately said to Carole that we had better go home and check out what was going on. When we were approaching our house, the road was blocked by Colorado Spring police who informed us that they were evacuating everybody in the area because the fire was at the top of the hills and the firemen were trying to keep it from coming down towards where our and other homes were. It reminded me very much of the Oakland Hills fire that we saw a few years earlier.

  There we were out on the street as evacuees with nothing more than the clothes we had on and unable to reach our new home. Our first job was to find Jesse and his family and we all finally met up at a Red Cross disaster center that had been set up. This was the beginning of a weeklong trek for us from various hotels to Breckenridge, CO where we stayed at a condo owned by a friend of Jesse and Michelle. We watched the fire from afar, hoping that the wind would drive it in another direction, and on Tuesday morning the wind shifted and it appeared we would not be in danger. But the people in charge of fighting the fire would not let us back until Sunday. Fortunately for all, there was no damage to our house although there was some dust and ash that had to be cleaned up. So, this was our introduction to Colorado: we had traded earthquakes in California for forest fires in Colorado.

I would like to say a few things about our new house. We are located at the base of Pikes Peak at an elevation of abour7000 feet. Thus, we really do live in the mountains. Our home, shown in the picture above, is what is called a Southwest style home in that the house looks much like homes in Santa Fe and other areas on New Mexico. We have three bedrooms, two on the second floor and one on the main floor that is used as a "music" room since all my CDs are in it as well as our television. Carole would use the small bedroom upstairs as her office for writing, and I had my computer on a desk in the living room. The house was built in 1996 and is in very good shape. It sits on a large lot of 25,000 square feet that contains semi-desert vegetation as well as cactus. We also have a variety of wild animals in our neighborhood, including deer, foxes, coyotes, bobcat, bears and even mountain lions. I have seen all but the mountain lions!

It has been hard to make new friends in Colorado. I think this was more important for Carole than for me since she is a much more social person than me. Fortunately, we met some people living close to us, Melody and Mark Bryan, and they have become strong friends. Carole and Melody immediately hit it off. They moved to Colorado from Southern California shortly after we did and had the same problem with the Waldo Canyon fire. Melody is a retired therapist and Mark is what I call a "space engineer" since he cannot discuss much of what he actually does because of security issues at this job. Carole made several attempts to contact people who were in the creative writing/fiction world but little came of this. One thing about Colorado Springs is that it is somewhat like a cultural desert in that there is little drama, music or art, and this is something we miss from life in the Bay Area.

    During the summer of 2013, our two oldest granddaughters came out to Colorado for a visit. As they got older, we started to take them on road trips when we were living in California: up to Mendocino, down to Hearst Castle. These trips were always great fun for all of us and when they started to drive, they could even help out on the road. In Colorado, I decided we would do one of our National Park trips. Carole and I had started to go to National Parks about five years ago and we had been to Crate Lake, Mount Lassen, Grand Canyon, Zion, Bryce Canyon Yellowstone and Grand Tetons. So for the summer,

Canyonlands National Park, Utah-July 2013

we drove to Northern Utah and visited Arches and Canyon Lands National parks, which were close to each other so this was a 2 for 1 trip. Since the girls were raised in the Baltimore area, I thought they should experience some of the natural wonders of the Western USA and none of us were disappointed by what we saw.

    Towards the end of 2013, Carole started to not feel very well. She was having pains that would come and go across her abdomen and also some pain in her upper neck region. We thought the latter might be related to the melanoma biopsy she had a couple of years before since we were told there could be nerve damage from the surgery. Carole never liked going to doctors and put off seeing anybody for some time. Some of this was related to the fact that we had never found a good general family practice physician in Colorado Springs. In early January of 2014, I finally convinced Carole to go to the doctor but it turned out our regular doctor was not available so we had to see someone else. Dr. Mitchell examined Carole and could not really come up with any diagnosis so he ordered some blood work for her. When we returned a few days later, he said there were some things that needed further checking and he wanted Carole to have an MRI of her abdomen.

    About a week later, we returned again for an appointment with Dr. Appleton. A few words about her: she was a young woman who had been in the military and only recently joined the Mountain View Medical Group. Her manner left one wondering about how she treated her previous patients--she was very direct and seemed to never have heard about bedside manner. Anyway, when she came into the examining room, she immediately blurted out that Carole had numerous tumors that were found on the MIR: liver, spleen, probably lung and upper spine. The most likely situation was advanced melanoma. Without saying much more, she suggested we talk with the palliative care people, i.e. hospice. I remember the two of us sitting in a state of complete shock, not even capable of crying over what we had just heard. We left quickly because there was just no point in trying to discuss anything further with Dr. Appleton.

At this point in time, I think I should let anyone reading this that this part of my story does not have a happy ending and, in fact, it constitutes the saddest part of my life. Carole died on Sunday, September 7, 2014 at 10 AM in our home in Colorado Springs.

After learning about Carole's cancer, we immediately searched for an oncologist to discuss her current health situation. The major cancer center in Colorado Springs is the Rocky Mountain Cancer Center and we were recommended to Dr. Maurice Marcus. In our first meeting with Dr. Marcus, he discussed several treatment possibilities and, unfortunately, also discussed the prospects that one might expect from any of them. Without going into details, we knew already from Daniel's situation many years before that there are no chemotherapy drugs that work in the case of melanoma. Surgery and radiation did not seem reasonable because of the wide spread of the cancer. Dr. Marcus did say that Carole should have an interventional biopsy to confirm that these tumors were from melanoma since it could be a recurrence of her breast cancer or some new cancer. Both of these seemed very unlikely but they should be ruled out.

During the month of February Carole's condition deteriorated rapidly. She was not eating well and was losing weight. Her energy level was also decreasing and we were getting concerned that she might fall. By the end of the month, it was clear Carole had to go into the hospital and I took her in on a Friday morning. Dr. Marcus came to see her a few hours later and he told us he was shocked at how poorly she had become, but he thought that with around the clock care, she would hopefully improve. It took about a week, but she was then well enough off to go home.

Dr. Marcus had been telling us about a new treatment that had just been approved by the FDA for advanced melanoma. It was found that melanoma cancer cells contained a mutant form of a protein, known as BRAF, which was absent in normal cells. Drugs had been developed that react specifically with the mutated BRAF and these were effective in inhibition of the cancer cells. Since we had no options available for Carole, we asked whether a genetic analysis of her cancer cells had the mutated BRAF protein, and the results were positive. I remember when Dr. Marcus called us to tell us she had the mutant form and we were so pleased at this finding. We then had to obtain the drugs and this turned out to be a major job because our insurance company, Humana, did not want to cover the cost, which was very high. They were arguing that this was an experimental treatment and not covered by our drug policy. There was a lot of back and forth with them from me and Dr. Marcus, and we finally obtained their approval. There were two different drugs required and they arrived in early March while Carole was still in the hospital, but they were immediately started.

Carole was taking 6 pills a day, two on one schedule and 4 on another, some before meals, some after meals, but we managed a schedule for her and it about 10 days, she started feeling much better, with her energy picking up and her appetite showing improvement. Also, there were no apparent side effects. It was like a miracle. After a few weeks, she was out taking hilly walks around Cedar Heights, something I thought I would never see again. This was a time when several of our friends from Berkeley came out to visit with her, usually for a weekend, and it picked up her spirits. Wonju , Abby and Ilana also came out to visit, and I was concerned because she had treated us so terribly for years, but even she was pleasant on the visits. Karin brought all of her children out to Colorado as well although they came one at a time since there was no way we could put all of them up.

When we started the BRAF medications, we were told that the effectiveness of the medication was found to diminish over time. In early studies, it had been found that the positive effects started to decrease at around six months, but that there were some individuals who remained on the drugs for up to two years. We were hoping for the best for Carole, but in July of 2014, she started to show the fatigue that she had seen before, and her appetite, which was never good, also took a turn for the worst. After consulting with Dr. Marcus, she went in for a scan to see what was going on. The results were not good in that the tumors were getting larger and her blood work also showed an increase in activity of the cancer cells.

As a last resort, we made a trip up to the Univ. of Colorado Medical School outside Denver to see Dr. Rene Gonzalez, who is recognized as a leading melanoma oncologist. We had seen him once before when we first arrived in Colorado but at that point Carole had only stage I melanoma and he did not feel he could do much for her. This time the situation was totally different, and we were hoping there was something on the investigational side of medications that might be appropriate. However, after a long discussion of her current state, he told us there was really nothing "out there" that was going to make a difference in her condition. He also brought up the hospice situation as a likely alternative.

When we returned home, Jesse, Karin and I all talked about what was next and we tried to bring Carole into the discussion but she insisted that whatever we decided would be fine with her. I think all of us realized at this point that there were no good medical options and we did not want to her to try any experimental, relatively untested drugs, and at this point we wanted her to be comfortable and not in pain in the time she had left. For me personally, this was the most wrenching decision I had ever made in my life, worse even than what I had gone through with Daniel. We had volunteered with the hospice group in the Bay Area for a number of years after I retired and were familiar with what they could for terminally ill patients and had done a little work with the local hospice group, Pikes Peak Hospice, when we came to Colorado Springs.

The hospice care Carole received over the month of August was outstanding. Carole was clearly declining and she had little energy and slept a great deal. At some point, I decided we needed to get her a downstairs bed so that she would not go up and down the stairs to our bedroom. I was afraid she would fall on the stars. Hospice provided a hospital bed that we put in our downstairs television/music room and I brought down another bed so I could sleep in the same room and help her in and out of bed. Around the first of September, she seemed even worse although she was not in a lot of pain. Over the first weekend in September, she started to be very agitated and confused and I called the hospice nurse to come in and see her. This was September 6th and the nurse examined her and told us that she was going to die soon and what she was going through was an indication of this. We were giving her morphine at this time and she was sleeping continuously. On the morning of September 7th, I was sitting next to her holding her hand when she passed away.

It is very difficult for me to write about this. However, I would like to finish this off. Carole had wanted to be cremated and to be buried next to Daniel's grave in Sunset View Cemetery. I had made contacted an organization known as Science Care for all of the necessary arrangements so there was little for me to do. I had organized a memorial service to be held at the Men's Faculty Club on Sunday, Nov. 2, 2014, and I went in a couple of days earlier for the burial and was joined at the cemetery by close friends from our years in Berkeley. The memorial service was very emotional for many of us. I asked Karin and Jesse to talk and also had all of our seven grandchildren involved in the program. There were also eulogies by Dorothy Witt, Mimi Toews, Daniel Marlin and Marshall Stoller, and each of these people had the most moving things to say about Carole.

    It would seem trivial to say that my life has changed forever since Carole died, but this is so true. We were married for almost 55 years and we functioned as a team. We did so many things together, starting when we were students at Antioch and cooperated on a joint history project. For a short note that was included in a publication by the hospice program, I mentioned that a bright light in my life has gone out. I know well what it is to grieve from Daniel's death, but losing your life partner is even more tragic. It is almost 18 months since she died, and I still have bad days where I go through all the wonderful things we did in our lives and then why did this have to happen. I know she did not want to die but she was suffering near the end and she told me one evening that she did not want to be this way and hoped she did die soon. These 18 months have been extremely difficult for me and the loneliness is sometimes overwhelming and I have to try to find ways to keep going.

    A few months after Carole died, I was going through her papers and I came upon a complete novel that she had written probably 20 years ago. I had previously put three of her novels on the Create Space website, a publishing concern run by Amazon. I followed this up with another publication that I entitled "The 'Complete' Stories" and finally a volume entitled "Poems." Her poetry is the most personal of all her writing, and deals with topics related to our life in Berkeley, her fight with breast cancer, and Daniel's illness and death.

Part IV. Final Remarks

I have taken you on a long journey of over 75 years and it is not yet over but it is time to stop my story. I think I have had a good life, with a truly wonderful partner, three children all of whom have done well in their lives, and a profession that has been rewarding to me for so long. But I have also learned that things do not always go as you wish they would and there is much that one cannot control in your own life. Losing our first born son was devastating, but the pain of losing Carole will never go away and I am not sure what the next five years will be like (I think it is a good idea to think in terms of 5 year periods when you get to be 75.) I am in good health and have a little Schnauzer dog (Hildie) that keeps me company. We take many walks and she patiently listens to everything I say when I talk about my life. Perhaps I should read this entire document to her so that she will understand me even better.

Hildie and Dick-December 25, 2015

Acknowledgements

    I would like to thank all of my children, my grandchildren and several friends for encouraging me to write this story, and particularly, Michelle and Jesse for reading through the final version and contributing critical comments and editorial corrections, of which there were many.